ALASKA FISHING ON A BUDGET

A FIRST-TIMER'S GUIDE TO ORGANIZING AND PLANNING AN ECONOMY SALMON FISHING TRIP TO THE LAST FRONTIER

BERNARD R. ROSENBERG

Frank Amato PORTLAND

Dedication

This guide is dedicated to "Flea" Benham from Anchorage.

His custom beauty vans took me to many places that I mention in this book. I drove his vans on highways, dirt roads, air strips, and over open fields. They took me through ice covered mountain passes and permafrost blacktop. They went through dust, mud, wind, rain, fog, and bugs. I put them on auto ferries and flat bed railroad cars. I slept in them, changed clothes in them, hung my tackle in them, and stored my fish in them. They took me from the congested bumper to bumper traffic in Anchorage, all the way to the unique loneliness of being in the middle of nowhere.

They never failed.

Acknowledgements

Among those who shared some of my experiences were my fishing companions Thomas Krause and Evan Duke. Special thanks are additionally expressed to Thomas Krause for the use of his skillful illustrations. Their organization (and their antics), complemented every day I spent in the Last Frontier. Thank you Tom, and thank you Evan.

As a first-time author, I never would have succeeded at compiling my thoughts had it not been for one more special friend. This is the one whose organization, patience, and computer skills assisted me in assisting you. Matter of fact this friend is so special that I married her. Thank you Gail, my lovely wife, and fishing partner for life.

Published in 2003 by Frank Amato Publications, Inc.
P.O. Box 82112, Portland, Oregon 97282
(503) 653-8108
www.amatobooks.com

Softbound ISBN-10: 1-57188-297-9
Softbound ISBN-13: 978-1-57188-297-4
Softbound UPC: 0-81127-00127-9

Book Design: Jerry Hutchinson

Printed in China
3 5 7 9 10 8 6 4 2

Contents

 # Purpose

Alaska Fishing on a budget is a guide designed for the average spin fisherman who has never been to Alaska and wants to fish for salmon and bring home the catch in the most cost efficient manner.

It is not designed for the purist fly-fisherman who adheres to the adage of catch-and-release. Nor is it designed for those who seek inner solace at the end of their pole while enjoying the comforts of a remote lodge. It is not for those who want to charter boats, charter bush planes, or charter helicopters. Nor is it for those who need a cook and a guide in order to have a good time. Alaska is full of all those services. And all of those services cost.

The most economical way to fish for salmon in Alaska is to fly into Anchorage, rent a vehicle, and fish from the highway systems out of town. As the roadways cross rivers and streams, the fishing areas they create become the least expensive way to catch fish in the entire state. Salmon are among Alaska's most popular and most abundant sport fishes. Fishing for salmon need not be a costly proposition so long as you are informed about the ways to go about it.

If you can handle a spinning rod, this book is for you. If you have ever dreamed about going to Alaska to fish for salmon, this book is for you. And if you have put it off because you thought you could never afford it, this book is especially for you. It can be done. All it takes is the experience of one who can show you the way.

I can show you the way.

If you are not into research, you soon will be. Gathering information, with the use of a personal computer, is essential to this guide being successful for you. The information highway that will lead you to the most cost-efficient way to fish from Alaska's highways is electronic. Accept it for what it is and take advantage of it. If you do, you will make your trip.

And now most importantly; if you are not accustomed to planning ahead, please reconsider and adopt a new point of view. To save money and create opportunity, you must plan ahead. If you do not, you are destined to get hooked and will undoubtedly pay through the nose. You might not even get a seat on your plane, your motel room, your campground spot, or even your rental vehicle. There is nothing casual about planning your first trip to Alaska. It is the early bird who catches the worm on every value trip up to the Last Frontier.

The primary focus of this book is to explain everything that is required to journey to and from Alaska in order to catch and bring home the state's most popular fish. Fishing Alaska is one thing. Getting there is another. This book links the two together. It is a guide to both the trip and the fish.

In addition, the book deals with salmon and crowds and how to play both of them. Things have changed in Alaska since I started fishing there some fifteen years ago. There were places then outside of Anchorage I could reach in an hour and fish totally alone as the sun rose into mid morning. Those days are gone. The streams are still there. The fish are still there. But now the crowds are there, too. Do not be dismayed. Crowds mean good fishing and fishing can be excellent in crowds. Not all of cost-efficient fishing has to revolve around this scenario. You will find many spots where you'll be moderately to completely alone, but generally that is not the norm. Count on being around people and accept them for what they are. They are fishermen just like you.

I wrote this book because there was a need for it. My experiences will point out to you how to save money and strategically plan an economical salmon-fishing trip based right out of Anchorage. I will show you what your options are concerning what to do with your catch from the time you pull it out of the stream until you put it on the plane. I will speak about the price of supplies, and demonstrate to you how you can save money by bringing in your own. My tips will identify two for one airfares, and even show you how you can fly free to Alaska. I will elaborate about the value season,

negotiating deals, renting vehicles, obtaining discounts, confirming space, and planning ahead. I address all of these important issues and even more.

I cannot begin to tell you how many inquires I have responded to from first time wannabes who have never fished the Great Land and who want to fish it as inexpensively as possible. Their questions ran just like the salmon; one after another after another and after another. They just kept coming and would not let up.

This book contains all those answers. It tells you where to go and when. It shows you what to use and how. I cover everything from what to wear, what to bring, how to pack, and how to fish. Every circumstance that surrounds you, from the moment you decide to go and up to the moment of your return, I discuss. Nothing is left out, and not a single stone is left unturned. And all of this information is presented with advice on how to save money along the way. It will lead you to both the trip and the fish. One does not occur without the other. That is why this guide was written.

I cannot ever guarantee a catch. That is why this streamside pursuit is called fishing and not catching. But I will tell you this. If there ever was a guy who could put you in the right spot, at the right time, and in the most cost efficient manner, I am your man.

 *Introduction*

My first trip to Alaska was a fluke. I scored a free round-trip air ticket on one of the major airlines and I had some free time during the summer to go visit someone. I picked Alaska only because my sister was temporarily living there. Her husband was a hot shot pilot and was stationed at Elmendorf Air Force Base right outside the city of Anchorage. Knowing that I could have a place to stay for free, I asked if I could come up and hang out. They accepted. Two weeks before my trip the pilot phoned me and said to bring my fishing gear because, "the Reds were running." I had no idea what he was talking about. I stuffed a couple of telescopic fishing poles and two older medium-sized spinning reels into my duffel. I knew nothing about Alaska and nothing about fishing for

A freezer full of frozen halibut could be your reward on your very first trip.

salmon. Boy, was I in for a surprise.

During that first trip I broke two inappropriate rods, burned out the bearings in two cheap reels, and ran through countless yards of monofilament. I rented hip waders that leaked, got stuck in tidal silt, and fell in cold water rivers more times than I wish to remember. I saw my tackle box drift away on an incoming tide. I was scared to death by a black bear sow and her two cubs on the bank of the very first stream I ever approached. I lost lures that were fished too slow, and sat frustrated on the river's edge because I failed to carry replacement equipment. I watched salmon snap my lines, and took the brunt of embarrassment as fishermen snapped at me for not following their unwritten rules. I learned everything the hard way.

But I caught fish. I caught a lot of fish. By the time I was ready to come home, the freezer in my sister's kitchen was stuffed full of zip-locked fillets of Red salmon, pink salmon, and chum salmon. I knew nothing about those species. I just figured that each and every one of them was a tribute to my success and that I should bring them all home. I paid out the nose for an approved airline carton, and paid even more for the dry ice to keep them cold. It wasn't until I started eating my prizes that I discovered that one was excellent, one didn't freeze well, and that the other one should have been left behind to feed to the dogs. No one ever told me.

This guide is put together to help spare you those ills. When I returned to Alaska two summers later to fish again, there was no one there to give me a place to stay and a free ride to the river. I had to pay for my own accommodations and my own car rental. There also were no free family meals. I had to buy my own food. I learned some things real fast. First, nothing is cheap in Alaska. And second, as the fish rise, so do the prices. Fishing Alaska can be really expensive for the uninformed and the unprepared. If you live in the lower 48 states and walk into a convenience store for a sandwich, cold drink, bag of chips, and a piece of fresh fruit for desert, you can throw the clerk a ten dollar bill and ask for change. Do that in some spots in Alaska and the clerk will ask you for yet another five dollars. That is what I mean by expensive.

Alaska can be cost efficient if you are informed. This guide will provide you with that information. It will show you how to get in, have fun, and get out again without your pocketbook taking a beating. It will show you how to plan your fishing so that you are not disappointed in your catch. And it will also inform you of what to do with your catch after you have succeeded in getting it. This guide will also teach you technique and etiquette, demonstrating to you how to respect the terrain you are visiting and the fish which you seek.

I have been returning to Alaska at least every other summer since that first trip in 1988. All it took was that one first time and I got salmon on the brain. I was hooked then and I still am hooked. Beware! What it did to me it might do to you.

Chapter 1

UNDERSTANDING SALMON

This is a simplified lesson in Salmon Biology 101. I am the teacher and you are the student. It goes like this; "Salmon lay eggs in freshwater streams. Eggs get fertilized then hatch. Hatchlings grow into tiny fishes and then head downstream to the sea. Years pass and tiny fishes feed and become big fishes. Big fishes then get the urge to reproduce and sniff out the same stream they came from in the ocean currents and head for it. Big fishes now swim upstream to lay eggs in the same spot, then die, and the cycle starts all over again. You catch them along the way. Any questions?"

It really is that simple. It happens all around the northern hemisphere of our globe. Salmon run those rivers and streams all the way from the Soviet Union, to Japan, to Norway, Finland, Iceland, North America, and on and on and on. Salmon are a cold water fish. Wait until you cut your first one with a knife. They do not even smell.

You will be just as surprised with the color of your fillets. Some are pale white to yellow, while others go all the way from bright orange to crimson red. It all depends on the species. What species you catch is dependent on when you are there and where you are. There are five species that run upstream in Alaska. They are the chinook, sockeye, coho, pink, and chum salmon. They all have nicknames. They all weigh differently. They all fight differently. They all eat differently. But there is one thing they all have in common and that is that all

Spawned-out and lifeless salmon deteriorate creating nutrients for the streams.

of them are heading your way and are thrilling to catch!

There are other commonalities. When they return from the sea and enter streams they are in peak condition. They are bright silver and firm of flesh. As they head upstream to spawn they all undergo change. New colors emerge. Jaws become distended and disfigured. Humps grow. Flesh deteriorates. The longer the fish is in fresh water, the poorer the quality of the flesh for you to eat. I learned that one the hard way when I grilled a crimson red sockeye salmon; it tasted like roasted cardboard soaked in cod liver oil. One learns from experience. Do not expect good quality if you have caught a brightly colored fish. Let it go.

All of these fish swim upstream in about the same manner. They swim in the deepest part of the water they are in. If there is a channel in the river or a furrow in the stream, that is where they will be while on their journey. They will swim until they get tired and then they will rest. They rest in deep pools or in the eddies behind boulders or beside sandbars in streams. Resting takes place anywhere the current lets up. Tired fish seek those places.

Clear-water streams and rivers actually allow you to see these fish, and during those times you can sight fish for them. That means you can cast your lure upstream ahead of them, and then retrieve your lure so that it passes directly under their nose and then they will bite it. It is an extremely effective technique. I remember sight fishing with a partner in Sheep Creek north of Anchorage

Lay a knife to a salmon and sometimes the color of its flesh will be crimson red.

using a highway bridge. He stood on the bridge and called out to me where to pitch my lures in deep pools. He could see the fish. I could not. I just followed his directions and cast where he told me to throw. It was a deadly combination. We nailed four chum salmon in less than a half hour. Look around when you're out there. Spotting for salmon is recognized as a technique for their capture. You will see many if you take the time to look.

Many Alaskan rivers and streams are not clear. They are fed by glacial melt and are quite cloudy. Though a map might indicate highway access and perhaps an opportunity, chances are that if fishermen are not there, nor should you be. (This is because in all probability, neither will be the salmon.) Besides, glacial melt areas are typically fast, cold, and dangerous. By-pass them.

Those five species of salmon run the rivers and streams all over Alaska. All five of these can be met by the economy angler who is staging a trip using Anchorage as the home base. Meeting them is dependent upon when you are there, and where you are located. Catching them is dependent upon your skills and equipment. Eating them becomes a matter of choice. All five are distinctly different.

CHINOOK SALMON

These are the largest salmon that migrate to spawn. They are the most powerful brutes of any salmon on Earth and the world record weighed 97 pounds. These massive fish have a deserving nickname. They are called kings. Due to their very strength, bank fishing opportunities for them for the value fisherman via highway access is slim. There are many areas in Alaska where you can wade in and fish for them with success, but getting to these areas is by bush plane or jet boat only and is costly. Centered from Anchorage, most fishing for kings typically involves a boat, a guide, and is a costly proposition. Kings are intensely regulated by the Department and Fish and Game, and require an additional fee that you must pay in order to fish and posses one. They require stronger and more specialized equipment, and sometimes catching them is even shut down due to emergency closure. Although they eat well, and are astounding to hook into and to land, I do not recommend the pursuit of king salmon for the first time fisherman. Generally, there just is not enough room in the crowds to play and land one your first time out.

Just because I advocate not going for them, it does not mean not catching them. There are always exceptions, and sometimes bank-fishing anglers off the highway system get lucky. But not often. Landing kings while highway fishing on a value trip is not the norm. It is an exception. However, you still might hook into one even though you are not fishing for a king. When you do, things will happen lightning fast, so pay attention.

When a sockeye hits, it will immediately turn around and head downstream. I had two on my stringer and was fishing for the third when a king struck my lure years ago on the Kenai River. Immediately, the line on my reel began to peel in a screeching run that was heading not down the river, but up the river and into the current. For a brief moment, a monstrous head reared up and exposed itself and then sunk back down. It was the largest head of any salmon I had ever seen alive and it was on the end of my line. In less than two minutes, it stripped my line all the way to the knot where it was tied to the reel and then broke it. I could not run with it, nor could I hold it. I was dumbfounded. I had never experienced so much power in my life.

If a king hits, you'll know it. You will probably be under equipped anyhow, and you won't be able to touch him. Do him a favor and do yourself a favor. Whip out your fillet knife and immediately cut your line. It saves you time, and your line, and that will save you money. Forget kings your first time up.

CHUM SALMON

These are the second largest salmon that migrate to spawn. Equipment I recommend in this guide will enable you to catch them. These salmon are abundant, and in many spots you fish, you'll hook up. Chum salmon are strong fish due to their very size. They are great fighters and leapers, and range in weight from the low to the high teens. They are thrilling to catch and unmistakable to recognize because this is the fish that undergoes the most staggering transformation when it enters fresh water. Banded colors appear on its sides. Its mouth transforms into a severely bent jaw

Chum salmon display vibrant colors as they go to spawn.

punctuated by protruding teeth. To the first timer, its face will almost look like a mad dog. It is little wonder that they then are affectionately known to locals as dog aalmon, chum dogs, or just plain dogs. It is a deserved nickname. And chum salmon do belong to the dogs. Alaskans feed them to their pets. You will generally catch them when they are not silver bright and they will not be good to eat. Take a victory photo and turn them loose.

Right now you are probably wondering what good is this guide. Of the five species that run, I have told you to omit two. There are only three left. It is these three that will transform the first time economy experience into the trip of a lifetime. It is these three that will especially please you. All can be eaten in the field with varying satisfaction. Two you should target to take back home.

PINK SALMON

This is the fish of your salvation. This is the most prolific and most abundant species in all of Alaska. It is the easiest to catch, and although it is the smallest in size, it bites just about anything you can throw at it. I have seen bays, rivers, and streams actually turn black because there were so many of them. If you could ever imagine so great a number of fish that they could displace water, this is the fish. Pinks are wonderful for the first timer. Get ready to enjoy them.

Pinks run strong during any calendar year that is divisible by two. No research I have read tells why, but accept it as fact. I have fished Alaska during odd calendar years. I was there. The pinks were not. If you want activity with pinks, plan your trip to take place in even numbered years.

Pink salmon are small. They range from four to eight pounds. As they enter fresh water, the males undergo a transformation and develop a severely pronounced hump on

Pilot (Rick Havard) shows why a pink salmon is sometimes called a "humpy."

their back. Thus they get their nickname. The locals refer to them as humpies. Pinks are fun fighters and worth every bit of your effort. They will run and they will jump, and it takes only moderate effort to land them. The experience is a delight for a child, or a spouse unused to fishing, and it is still good for you as well. If you want to see smiles, catch a pink.

The problem is, since there are so many of them, pinks sometimes get in the way of the other salmon you seek. They wind up taking your lure before other salmon, and for some fisherman the pink is a pest. That probably accounts for the phrase, "Humpies from hell!" You will hear it from those who do not want them. A pink salmon can evoke that kind of response.

Pinks do not freeze well, so do not bring them home. But freshly caught, they are great on the grill, steamed, smoked, or broiled. It is a favorite fish to can. The key to enjoying pinks is to eat them now. Do not let the locals tell you to cast this salmon aside. You might consider what I do with mine.

I harvest pinks outside of Anchorage in Bird Creek, and in Hope at Resurrection Creek. Those two areas are affectionately known to me as Pink City. I catch pinks not so much to eat them, but rather to harvest the eggs in the females. Salmon roe caviar is a delicacy. A tiny store bought jar of about two ounces will fetch almost $15.00. An average-size female pink will yield almost six ounces in eggs. You do the math. How anyone can think this fish is a pest is beyond me. And I cannot begin to tell you the smiles this fish brings after I get done with it. Return to your campground space and offer freshly caught fillets of pink salmon to perfect strangers who do not fish and watch what happens. You will make friends in no time. Pinks are wonderful for any first timer. If you can schedule them to be included as part of your first Alaskan experience, I would recommend it.

Now I am down to the very core of what successful and inexpensive salmon fishing is all about. There are only two species left for me to explain. Target either one of these, or better yet, target both your first time up. You can eat any of the two in the field with unrivaled satisfaction. These are the ones that freeze the best. These are Alaska's two remaining salmon that are the biggest challenge for you to land. These are the two you will talk about and always remember. They are the coho and the sockeye salmon.

COHO SALMON

Coho salmon are Alaska's best fighters. When hooked, it does not matter which way the current runs. The coho will leap, thrash, and run in any direction it cares to fight. It is a thrilling fish to catch. It lasts long in fresh water, and even though its silver sides will have begun to turn a dull red, it is still good to eat. Lay a knife to the sides of a coho salmon and the flesh will reveal itself as bright orange.

Since cohos remain silver colored for so long, its nickname is adeptly configured to its hue. It is referred to as a silver. silvers are a late-summer to to a mid-fall fish. Most runs in Alaska do not even start until near the end of July, and then continue to run into October. This fish averages about ten to twelve pounds.

Silvers are among one of the salmon species that will actively feed on bait during their migration. You can

A pair of silver salmon contrast in color due to their length of time in the river.

Tom Krause holds a nice silver salmon.

catch them with spoons and flies, and you can catch them with bait. A heavy spoon is a killer lure for a silver, but a ball of salmon eggs works equally as well. Egg-sac portions are wrapped with a piece of fine mesh fabric, and then are stuck onto hooks and weighted down with lead. The presentation lays on the bottom until a silver picks it up and then the fight is on. Eggs are just as deadly as lures.

I was fishing Montana Creek north of Anchorage one season for silvers. I happened to walk across a railroad trestle and look down. There, holding in the pools created in the eddies behind the bridge pilings, lay three fine fish. I had the lures, but there was no way to present them to the silvers because of obstructions. A bait ball would be perfect. In that limited space, I knew I could cast ahead and let the current roll the presentation directly in their faces. Problem was, I had no eggs.

I noticed an older couple downstream from the bridge. They were filleting their catch and their day was over. They had done well. I walked up to them and politely asked if they wouldn't mind giving up some roe. They did. Now I had my bait. I also had hooks and lead with me, but no fabric meshing. I needed something to wrap those eggs on the hook, or those three salmon I had discovered were going to stay there. The next question took a lot of nerve.

"M'am," I said, "I know this seems absurd, but if I gave you a five dollar bill would you allow your husband to cut the tops off your panty hose that I am assuming you are wearing underneath those waders?"

That old time couple just looked at me and laughed. They knew what I wanted and why I wanted it. (I told you I had salmon on the brain.) That kind of a question proved it.

I returned to those pools and put together three bait balls and rolled all three. Thirty minutes later the Alaska Railroad thundered by atop its trestle. As the day tourists stuck their heads outside their windows and waved and cheered, I held up over 30 pounds of salmon for everyone to see. That moment was so great even the engineer blew his horn. I will never forget it. Alaska is full of those kind of experiences and each trip never ceases to amaze me. It is that kind of a place.

You bought this book to save money and I told you I would show you how to fish for salmon in the most cost-efficient manner. The least expensive fishery that you can ever put together is fishing for Silvers. Silvers continue to run into October. September is when the tourist season in Alaska ends and the value season begins. Crowds thin out and fall has arrived. As the leaves drop, so do the prices. Vehicle and hotel rentals can sometimes be reduced as much as 50 percent. The savings are obvious. A budget-minded angler can do no better than targeting a trip based on the information I have just shared. If you want value, there it is.

SOCKEYE SALMON

I have saved the best for last. There is no better eating salmon in all of Alaska than this fish. Sockeye eats best because its fat content is the highest. There is no better fryer, baker, smoker, poacher, or griller than the sockeye salmon. It is the most revered and the most highly prized flesh in all of Alaska's salmon species. Therein is the problem; everybody knows it.

When you fish for sockeye, expect crowds. Crowds will show up just as readily as the fish. Sockeye will be everywhere. People will be everywhere. It is unavoidable for the economy based angler who uses the highway to access sockeye fishing areas outside of Anchorage. So does everybody else. You cannot fight it. You must join it.

The locals have nicknamed sockeye salmon reds. This is due to the intense scarlet coloring of the male as he spends time in fresh water. His head will turn deep green. His body will turn bright red. Of all salmon transformations, this one is the most beautiful. These fish average eight to ten pounds in weight. They are formidable fighters, and when hooked, will immediately turn and head downstream. As they run downstream, so will you. It is quite the norm to see fishermen chasing down this prize.

Reds do not feed. Reds will not take bait. Reds just forge ahead. In some places there can be thousands of them, and I mean thousands. As these fish begin to enter the freshwater drainage where you will be fishing, they are monitored by the Department of Fish and Game and are counted by sonic devices. Red salmon return to some parts of Alaska in two distinct and separate migrations. This is especially true south of Anchorage. The first run occurs during early June. The second run appears almost five weeks later near the end of July. These runs can be so profuse that people joke about the upcoming Red Army. It is quite an event and a double opportunity. The by-product of this migration is a phenomenon known as combat fishing.

In combat fishing, the highway angler will line up almost shoulder to shoulder with other fishermen. The number of fishermen can vary, depending upon the time of year and location, and can range from dozens to the hundreds. All of them will be casting lures upstream and retrieving them as they drift downstream. It is a rhythm of casting and winding, plopping and plunking, all in the hope that their spoon or fly will literally bump into the face of an approaching salmon. When that happens, the fish will instinctively strike at the lure just to get it out of the way. That is when the fun begins.

A struck red immediately leaps out of the water. The lucky fisherman then immediately yells out, "Fish on!" The hooked salmon then surges downstream. Nearby neighbors immediately reel in their lines and step aside to give the fisherman an opportunity to land his prize. In concept, that is how it is supposed to work. Most of the times, and quite amazingly, it does. People catch a lot of fish in this manner when things go smoothly. I have seen many a happy fisherman while fishing in crowds. But sometimes, things go wrong. In crowded conditions you can also expect heartbreaking disappointments.

A red will snap a light line set too tight like the crack of a rifle. He will also strip line off a reel just like a king if a drag is set too loose. And I guarantee he will go stark raving nuts if you touch him by the tail if you attempt to net him other than head first. Couple this with spit out lures, slipping on rocks, undoing tangles, and having six anglers with fish on at the same time, and combat fishing can reach new heights of confusion,

frustration, argumentation, and excitement. It is quite an experience for any angler, let alone a first timer, but reds are well worth the fight. Step in there and do battle for them.

Those are the five species. My favorite time to fish is the third week of July through the first week of August in the even numbered calendar years. Selecting those specific times has enabled me to enjoy pinks and chums, and to bring home silvers and reds all in one shot. Now that you understand salmon, I will point out just what exactly you will have to do to in order to get them.

The author displays a fine catch of red salmon.

Chapter 2
MAKING THE COMMITMENT

Congratulations! You have taken that all important first step. For whatever the reason, if you are reading this now, you have an interest in going to Alaska to fish, and you have a desire about how to go about it yourself without getting skinned to death. I am glad you are here.

There is nothing casual about going to Alaska if you plan on being cost efficient and having a successful catch. Timing is everything. Timing affects everything you do. From the moment you book your incoming flight, to the moment you arrive back home, time affects everything around you. In Alaska, time regulates tides, sunlight, runs of fishes, hotel rates, highway driving conditions, crowds on the river's edge, fish processing opportunities, campsites, accommodations, charters, bookings, and on and on. It is endless. Do not fight it. Take advantage of it.

Time is your enemy if you do not plan ahead. You are going to plan ahead. A first timer who has chosen to fish Alaska should be starting about a year ahead of time. I am not kidding. The sooner you decide to go, the sooner you can get time on your side. I will give you an example.

One season I booked a trip to Kodiak. I had three friends who had committed to take this trip with me. Therefore, we were a party of four. We were there in July. Eleven months before July, I engaged a skipper of a charter service to book his boat for a one day fishing trip. He was intrigued that I should make so early an inquiry. His calendar was wide open. His boat normally rented for $800.00 per day. My skipper wanted me to book his boat for another day. "No way, he said, "should anyone ever come to this wondrous island without at least giving it two days worth of fishing at sea. Book my boat for two days, and if you do, I will throw in an extra day for only $500.00 and your party will save three hundred bucks."

I booked it. And that is what I mean by getting time on your side

The author and friend pose with a catch of silver salmon and black rockfish while on a charter.

and having it work for you. In this circumstance, early commitment provided me with the bargaining power I needed to reduce costs. Early commitment provided an opportunity to negotiate price. Let me give you another example of how early commitment can work for you.

After we left Kodiak, one member of my party had to return home. The other three of us had planned to fish the confluence of the Kenai and Russian rivers. I had scheduled this trip at the projected peak of the second sockeye salmon run. When the Reds are running, this area becomes the single-most crowded and congested highway bank fishery in the entire state of Alaska. If you don't plan on it ahead of time, forget it. Campgrounds are filled up, parking places are used up, and there is no spot to stick your vehicle and spend the night within miles.

But not so with us; we were there for three nights in one of the state's most congested campgrounds, and our guaranteed camping space was one of the nicest and nearest walking spots to the river. While dozens of cars waited hours in line for the skinny chance of finding a space that wasn't even available or close in, we just drove to the front of the line and showed them our printed prepaid reservation and slipped in just as gently as a leaf riding on the water. Had it not been for an early commitment we never could of done it. That reservation was made more than a half year ahead of time. For economy and opportunity, it is the early bird who gets the best worm in Alaska. I have mentioned this before. Never forget that all-important fact.

A campfire blows smoke during a late afternoon at a campsite on the Russian River.

Making up your mind to go is your first step. Certainly it is much cheaper to travel with friends than to go it alone, because with friends you can split costs. A trip with two to four persons is perfect. Sharing the costs with friends is the smart approach. But either way is do-able. Just decide to go, then get on with it.

FLYING FREE TO ALASKA OR FLYING HALF PRICE

An airline ticket to Anchorage from just about anywhere is a costly proposition. Alaska is located near the top of the world. You are not. I will pay to get to Anchorage if I have to. However, most times I do not have to pay at all. I fly free. Here is how it works.

As soon as you decide you are going, consider to make this all-important first move; get a credit card that offers you premiums every time you use it. Select a card that gives you free air miles as that premium. Use the card to rack up air miles, and in the future, you will fly to Alaska for free.

I come from a household of two persons. We charge our gasoline, our food, our entertainment, our expenses, and anything else we run across on one single credit card. Before we secured that card, we used to pay by cash, by check, by gasoline credit card, by department store cards, and by bank credit cards. Those methods of payments rewarded us with little or nothing. All they did was pay bills. We still generate bills, but now we do it on a single card that generates premiums every time we use it. Each dollar we charge, we pay off at the end of the month and pay no finance fees. For every dollar we

charge, we are awarded one air mile that is placed in our mileage account.

Each year my wife and I spend enough money that we qualify for two round trips of airfare anywhere in the continental USA including Alaska. I have not paid for a flight north in over ten years. I fly free to Alaska almost every time. There is no cheaper way to get to Alaska then by not paying to get there, period.

This same credit card offers many first time applicants an inducement to enroll. They offer a complementary companion air ticket voucher that can be given to a friend. Two can go for the price of one.

Remember that trip to Kodiak I was telling you about? Two members in that party flew at half price. Instead of paying $800.00 each to fly and return from the top of the world, both paid half that amount. They cut their costs in two. They took my advice and phoned some of the major credit card companies and found one that offered a companion fare inducement for enrollment. All it took was a little of their time and some toll-free phone calls. What is good for the goose is good for the gander. What they did, you can do. And what I did, you can do. Anyone who is paying full fare to fly to the Great Land is missing the boat. The sooner you get on board, the sooner you will save.

Now that you have decided to go, it is time to get busy. You have got a lot of questions and they deserve a lot of answers. You now need information. In the next section, I will show you how to get most of it for free.

Chapter 3

UTILIZING RESOURCE MATERIAL

There is plenty of information available to help you plan this trip. Most of it is free. Some of it you will have to pay for, but only one purchase item is really required. Information will come to you in two ways; printed materials or electronic materials. The informed fisherman will use both.

FREE PRINTED MATERIALS

The best way to begin to amass free printed information about Alaska is to take a trip to your auto club. These associations have free guides and tour books and maps relative to your trip. How anyone could operate a vehicle on our highway systems without becoming an auto club member is beyond me, but if you are not a member, at least ask around until you find one of your family members or friends who is, and then ask them to pick this information up for you.

The tour book is critical. It provides you with your basic start up information and contacts to make in order to get more free information. It will contain toll-free numbers and mailing addresses dealing with fishing regulations. It will contain information about recreation areas that describe the parks in which you can stay. It will describe to you in detail the hotels in Anchorage and accommodations in other towns and what you will have to pay for them. Maps are in there. Coupons are in there. Advertisers are in there. The tour book is your basic orientation to your trip and it is free. Get it and begin using it.

When you do unfold your map of Alaska and look at the state, you will be amazed at how immense this area really is. Alaska is not ranked first in size in the USA by mistake. An area of 586,412 square miles is quite formidable. But now look at the highway system. You will immediately notice there is not a lot to it. The simple fact of the matter is that Alaska's highway system is quite small. What is there, is either two-lane blacktop or gravel road. There is no interstate system at all.

Look closely at Anchorage. This is your gateway city. Gateway means this is the city you fly in to and return from. Anchorage is the key player in your trip. You will shop in Anchorage. You will stay the night in Anchorage. You might even have fish processed in Anchorage. Anchorage in the summer is high season. It is loaded with tourists. You are one of them.

Look at the highways that run out of Anchorage. There are only three of them. One goes to the south and splits. One goes to the north. And the other one goes to the west and then bisects another highway that runs in two directions. Your economy fishing trip will take place on and off these highways. You will not have to go far to get a lot. And I am not just talking about the fish. The view from these highways will be drop dead gorgeous. Expect to have your breath taken away. Just about every city or town on those highway systems will have a chamber of commerce. Since Alaska is a state whose economy is dependent upon tourism, I can assure you that they will have plenty of free information they will send you if you ask for it. Information that is not available in print will be available electronically via computer. Getting that information is easy.

PRINTED MATERIALS FOR PURCHASE

There are other hard copy materials that will assist you in your planning. For anyone who is considering the trip, I would recommend these investments. What you will get in return for what you will pay, far outweighs the price of either of these two items. I suggest you consider purchasing both, but at the very least, you must purchase one to assist you.

The first item is a subscription to *Alaska Magazine*. This monthly publication will keep you in touch with the goings-on outdoors in the state you are about to visit. It is a very personal magazine with outstanding articles and essays, and is richly complemented with superior photography. There is plenty of advertising, and it is through your communication with some of these advertisers that you might enrich your journey. Please consider electing to subscribe to this magazine the moment you commit yourself to your trip. You will not be disappointed.

The second item is the softcover book, the *Milepost*. *Milepost* is a staggering atlas of information. It takes apart Alaska's highways and gravel roads mile by mile, and tells you what is available in services, nature, and fishing opportunities each and every mile you travel. Since you are going to be on the highway, you will want to take advantage of such a publication. I ran Alaska's highways

six years before I bought this book. I had no idea what I was missing until I read it. Now, I miss nothing. Nor should you. I strongly recommend that you purchase this book since it will be critical for you to know exactly what the road holds in store for you. This book will tell you everything. You should be able to find the *Milepost* at any major bookstore.

ELECTRONIC INFORMATION

There is no better pulse on our ever-changing world than the computer. The opportunity to use it to access information is astounding. Your computer will allow you to view opportunities via the Internet and secure them. It will allow you to compare services and purchase them. It will give you up to the minute details on the run of the fish and the weather. It is absolutely invaluable for planning your first trip, or any other return trip.

The key to understanding how to research Alaska by computer is by using the right keywords in any search. Put your computer on a good search engine, type in the right keywords, and information will come flying out at you like all those Alaskan mosquitos you have been needlessly worrying about.

Take for instance that magazine I suggested you subscribe to. I gave you no address, no phone number, and no website. In short, I gave you nothing except a name and a suggestion. If you type in the words "Alaska Magazine" on your computer's search engine, it will immediately pop up. Included in its site will be a picture of the magazine, examples of articles, rate information, address, toll-free number, testimonials, and even a complementary trial issue. That is what I mean by information. There is nothing faster and nothing more up-to-date than information that comes your way via computer.

Because I want to keep my assistance timely, I will never offer up a phone number, or an address, be it either written as a street or posted as a site, for you to use. These things can change. It is by far better for you to understand that you need only to search the concept via a few keywords in order for you to get the current information you will need to assist you.

Thirty seven sentences ago I told you that getting information about a

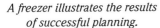

A freezer illustrates the results of successful planning.

city or town on Alaska's highway system was easy. With your computer, you can visit any area ahead of time and determine if that area is interesting or important enough for you to visit and fish. All you have to do is look at your highway map for city or town names, and then add "Alaska" afterwards and you will be bombarded. Type in "Anchorage, Alaska" and you will see what I mean. Even the tiny towns might have something going. It is up to you to explore, so start exploring.

Keywords always provide the successful angler with key information. It was no fluke that led me to pick the third week of July through the first week of August as my prime time to fish outside of Anchorage during the even numbered calendar years. That important decision was made based on investigative research. I typed in "Alaska fish reports" and wound up on the website of the Department of Fish and Game for the state. Cruising the site enabled me to gain access to historical archives on the runs of fish. I was able to pull up regions and reports. I cross indexed information and compared one area to another. I read of fishing trends and fishing forecasts. I identified species and rivers. In short, I did my homework. I then came to the conclusion of where to go and when. Luck is not what fills my cooler every time I return home from Alaska. Skill fills it.

ONLINE NEWSPAPERS

I read the *Anchorage Daily News* five days a week on my computer. Keeping up with the local news keeps me abreast of what is going on in the area of my interest. Reading the newspaper gives me a feel for where I am going, and helps give me a greater understanding for the strangers I am going to meet. If I read about their issues, I get to talk to them about what concerns them. Being informed never hurt anyone, and a daily newspaper can give you information that is relevant. There is no added cost to read a newspaper online, it is free.

ONLINE MESSAGE ROOMS

Fishermen love to talk. Alaska has fishing forums where you can post messages and get answers. Fishermen advertise localized services and some even put together swaps. This even allows you the opportunity to make friendships with some people who actually live in the areas you plan to visit. The opportunities from a good site that has a message board are endless.

When I went to Kodiak that summer, I wanted an opportunity to smoke my own fish and bring them home. I knew I needed a smoker and a supply of wood in order to do this. I also knew I would have access to neither when I was there. But I am also an artist, and I happen to sculpt salmon out of clay. Before that trip, I posted a message that indicated I would be willing to trade a piece of my salmon sculpture for the use of a smoker and a supply of wood to any Kodiak resident. A local took me up on it, and a swap was accomplished. There was no fee to post this message online. It too, was free.

Your computer will be a major player that contributes to information essential to your trip. You have motels to book. You have an itinerary to develop. You have a vehicle to rent. You need to learn about salmon regulations. All of this information awaits you at the play of your fingertips and the push of a button. And the nice

The author holds a sea-bright king salmon caught during a charter.

thing is none of it costs any more than what you pay for your monthly cable. It is out there and you've already paid for the right to retrieve it, so start retrieving. I wish you well on your searches. May all your deals blow as sweet as the smoke that cured my salmon.

BUILDING FILES

As you request information, or as you print information, you soon will discover that you will need a suitable place to keep it all in order. A drawer full of brochures, printed data, pictures, tour books, and maps will quickly stuff itself if you are taking my advice. You might want to consider building some sort of file for what comes your way in hard copy. Hard copy is enjoyable. It always gives me pleasure to review and look at my information about Alaska before I go. It is kind of like having two vacations; one is the plan and the other is the trip. Both are always worth my time. Both will be worth your time.

On the other hand, electronic files are easy to store because they do not take up space. Keep records and bookmarks of all the significant things you discover and file them in your computer. You will be surprised how quickly this will grow, and even though something might seem unusable for the moment, you might wind up coming back to it.

REVIEWING YOUR DATA

Just as it is up to you to gather information, so it is equally up to you to study it. Only by studying will you be able to make comparisons and then draw them into conclusions that will benefit you. Two of the most important conclusions that you will decide will be when are you going, and where you are going. The next two sections deal exactly with finding those answers.

The author and a friend spend time planning for success.

Chapter 4
TIMING YOUR TRIP

When you come up to the Great Land you are going to have to deal with how much time you have and how can this time be used best. Those are the two crucial factors that face you; length and date. It should go without saying that the longer you are up and out there, the greater it will cost; but then again the greater will be your opportunity to catch fish. It should also be noted that the shorter your stay, the less will be your cost; but then again, your opportunity to catch fish will be less. It sounds like a dilemma, but it is not. It is only an equation.

LENGTH OF AN IDEAL TRIP

My recommendation for the first time angler is a nine day trip. This gives the fisherman a full week of the Alaskan experience and two travel to get there and return. Nine days is perfect for the first timer. You get to spend a week in the bush and you can fish your heart out. A week allows you time to cross the highway systems as you seek salmon. A week gives you time to investigate and explore. A week gives you the opportunity to meet Alaskan people and enjoy their friendships. A week on the road is perfect.

Your vehicle rental is best figured on a weekly rate. Shorter days mean higher costs per day. This is yet another reason for the nine day trip. If you can afford to stay longer, then by all means do so, but at least give yourself one full week to enjoy this great place. If you do not have nine days it certainly does not mean you are out of luck. It only means you will have to be a little more careful with your time and how you use it. Nine days is only my suggestion based upon my experiences. I certainly have been happy with nine days. It is my hope that you will be happy, too.

All vacation trips to Alaska must include travel days. You have to count them as part of your trip. It takes me twelve hours to reach Anchorage from my home, and I easily consume a whole day in just getting there. I use up another whole day on my return. In all probability, so will you. Include two days in your travel calendar just for transportation. And speaking of calendars, use one. Get your hands on a calendar that covers the year you intend to go, and use that in your planning as you target your fishery dates. It is an invaluable tool.

If you only have a week off, I still would advise renting a vehicle and doing a highway road trip. This would still be the most cost efficient way to go. A week would give you up to five days in the streams, and you could still fish well if you knew where the fish were. The same would hold true if you only had six days, or five, or at the minimum, four. But four days is where I will call it quits. Why anyone would want to invest the travel time and money to come all the way to Alaska and chance a fishery for only two days is beyond me, but even then it can still be done. Even fishing one day in Alaska is better than fishing no days in Alaska. I will show you how you can do that trip and you will not even have to rent a car.

THE ONE-DAY FISHERY

Although I do not endorse bush plane services due to high cost, a one-day flight during a short stay is worth mentioning. You can fish Alaska on only a three day vacation. It is chancy, but it can be done. Here is how. Direct your research toward fly-in fishing. You will discover that there are flying services in Anchorage that will pick you up from your hotel for free. They will transport you to their business location, and then fly you to a designated area where the fish are running. Your pilot will drop you off, and you will fish unguided for about six to eight hours. Your pilot will then return and pick you up. When you arrive back in Anchorage, you will again be transported back to your hotel for free.

You will be absolutely in the wild and away from any road. Your flight will be a thriller, and they will put you on the fish. You will be away from the crowds, completely. You will be in for a superior adventure. This is the stuff fishermen dream about, and you can buy into this experience for around $200. Bear in mind that if the weather is bad, pilots do not fly. Your one-day fishery could get washed away.

Even then you could have an alternate plan and still fish. So long as you have researched the right run at the right time, you could still rent a car and reach a fishery within hours of Anchorage and fish in the rain. Rain never stops the fish. You can catch salmon regardless of the weather. So long as you get there when they are there, they are yours.

Although I have done a one-day bush plane unguided fly-in, I have never planned it as part of a three day vacation because I knew I would have to use up two of the days in order just to get there. Add in two nights in Anchorage, and the costs mount up. If I had to do it, I definitely would schedule it during the start of the value season and target the Silvers. I suppose I have got enough

salmon on the brain to consider this alternate plan, but as of yet it has not happened. I do fantasize about it, though. Perhaps for me, this option is only a matter of time.

DATE OF AN IDEAL TRIP

I have already twice indicated the dates I consider ideal that are suited to my calendar, and I have shared with you some reasons why. My choice was easy. I had plenty of flexibility. All I had to do was to choose the right time and then show up. If you are flexible you get to do this. You can show up at selected rivers and streams on the highway system outside of Anchorage and catch salmon from the month of May through the month of October. That last sentence is so powerful that you should go back and read it again. Please do that.

That type of statement also can be very misleading. If you take it at face value without thinking much about it, chances are you are going to come up empty handed and you will check your cooler home in the same condition. The salmon are around during that entire time, but as the months change, so do the runs and so do the species. Rivers full of salmon become rivers devoid of salmon, and streams once empty become streams now filled with fish. Things change. Water temperature can affect a run. Water depth from the rains can effect a run. Commercial fishing can effect a run. Tides can effect a run. Even biologists can affect a run. Let me give you a classic example.

Years ago, fish biologists introduced a migration of silver salmon into Bird Creek outside of Anchorage. This creek had supported only natural runs of chum and pink salmon, but due to tourism-and the fish needed to support the industry, silvers were added. An artificial run was created and it was successful. Popularity and fishing pressure on this creek increased dramatically.

One year during a spawning season, the biologists happened to release too many silver fingerlings. When they matured and returned several years later, their numbers were so great that the Department allowed the daily quota to be almost doubled. When the word got out, the results were catastrophic.

Fishermen and salmon were everywhere. Cars, trucks, and recreational vehicles cluttered and overflowed the parking areas. The abundance of people impacted the immediate area with litter, accidents, arguments, and so much foot traffic that people beat the edges of this fragile creek almost to death. There were just too many fish and too many fishermen.

The Department has since corrected this mistake, and now more carefully measures the release of Silvers in that area in order to limit the impact of people. At one time the state had even considered releasing King salmon into that creek, but realizing the nightmare it would create, that bad dream never happened. This is what I mean when I mention that things may change.

Nevertheless, your optimum research comes from Alaska's Department of Fish and Game. Visit their site and get familiar with it. Many things that you will need to know are there. They will send you free materials that will greatly assist you. I cannot stress the importance of this site other than to have brought it up, once again. Just be sure and understand that nothing is carved in stone. Be flexible. A week in the bush provides you with that opportunity to move to where the fish might be.

AN INFLEXIBLE TRIP

Not every first-time angler gets to pick a date to fish Alaska. Some vacation dates are already scheduled, and your circumstance might be the one that says this is the only available time for you to go. Although outwardly you might think this works against you, in honesty, it does not. If you look at what limitations cause, it actually will make planning your trip all the more easy.

Since your date is locked in, all you have to do is review the fishing reports centered around those dates. Ignore all the others. The only thing you are looking for is where the salmon are forecast to run during the time you are there. Your planning is the easiest of all. The fish are either scheduled to be there, or they are not. Plan your trip if they are. Do not plan a trip if they are not. It couldn't be simpler.

PUT TIME ON YOUR SIDE

As soon as you have determined your time slot, make your airline reservations. Just because the destination is remote, do not be lulled into the false sense of security that you have plenty of time to get a seat. More and more people travel to Alaska every year. Summer is the peak season. Airline seats fill fast. And if you are traveling with any type of voucher, like a free pass or a two for one companion fare, they fill even quicker due to the limited space deliberately imposed by the air carriers to limit voucher usage. Make your airline reservations to Alaska ten months ahead of time. I told you there was nothing casual about planning your first trip and I meant it. If you are planning a year ahead, a reservation made two months after you have amassed information is completely in order.

I target the fisheries in the next section. I will let you know generally where the salmon will be. Expect occasional crowds.

Chapter 5
TARGETING FISHING LOCATIONS

Finding your fish can be as easy as one, two, three. That is because that is the number of major highway systems you confront that go in and out of Anchorage. As mentioned already, there are only three of them. One goes just to the north. One goes to the south and splits. And one then goes to the west and intersects. All three have different names. All three offer different terrain. All three are subject to different vehicle pressure. One of the highway systems is lonely, and offers some good fishing opportunities that are far away. Another of the highways is moderately used, and offers great fishing opportunities that are not too distant. And the last of the highway systems is congested, and offers many excellent fishing opportunities that are all over the place.

The best way for you to get an orientation of these highways is to have your road map unfolded as I share information with you. My intent is to give you a generalized account of what these highways are like. Each of the highways maintains a system of milepost markers on it. At any given time, you will then know the actual number of miles you are away from any major city or town that connects to it.

Speaking of mileposts, it is now time for you to go back to that supplemental piece of printed information that I recommended you to buy. The softcover book, the Milepost, should be used by you to help you target your fishery locations. The book reveals almost every single fishing spot that you can reach by car. The book also reveals every single campground or motel accommodation that is near those spots. Since you are a road fisherman, this is your road

Alaska's salmon streams are streams of beauty.

guide. That is why I consider it invaluable. You should be using it.

There will be two types of fishermen are on the road. One will be the type who likes to camp. The other will be the type who likes to stay in a motel. Those who camp will save money. Those who stay in a motel will spend money. It is a personal choice, but the three highway systems will accommodate either of you so long as you plan and reserve ahead of time. I prefer to use a combination of the two; I camp a few days and nights, and then duck into a motel to freshen up, and then camp again.

Do not think that because you might drive far from Anchorage the crowds will be less. This is not the case at all. People are all over, especially during the peak of the salmon runs during midsummer. But on some spots on these highways you will not even see a soul. It all depends upon where you pull off and what little nook you discover. Even a crowded stream can sometimes open up if you take the time to hike away from the easy-access areas. That is all part of the Alaskan experience and it is yours for you to discover.

Roadside salmon fishing from all three of these major systems can vary.

Runs of fish are rated due to the numbers of salmon present at selected locations. Ratings are commonly recognized as poor, fair, good, and excellent. I will omit all areas that are poor, seldom mention areas that are fair, and point out all areas that are good to excellent. Since I do not recommend a first timer to target kings, they will not be included at any location.

THE GLENN AND RICHARDSON HIGHWAYS

These are the lonely highways that offer up some good fishing far away. Vehicle pressure on these highways is light. You catch them by leaving Anchorage on Highway #1 to the north of the city. About 42 miles later it bears to the right to the town of Palmer, and becomes known as the Glenn Highway. It then runs west 147 miles to the town of Glennallen. From Glennallen it splits and becomes Highway #4. It is then known as the Richardson Highway as it runs 120 miles south to the Port of Valdez. Driving these highways is a one-way run. That means you have to turn around and drive back the way you came. There is a ferry service available in Valdez that circumvents this, but I will not suggest it due to the cost. You

Glenn and Richardson Highways
Salmon Fishing Forecast

Location	Species	Timing	Rating
Moose Creek	Silvers	Late August to early September	Fair
Klutina River	Reds	Late June and all of July	Good to excellent
Little Tonsia River and Tonsia River Confluence	Silvers	Late September to early October	Fair to good
Allison Point	Pinks	July	Good
	Silvers	Late August to early September	
Robe River	Silvers	Mid-September	Good

will travel a long way on these roads to reach fish and then have to travel a long way to get back.

Most of these highways run through valleys, mountains, or glacial areas. They are far from towns of any size, and the surrounding terrain is wild and spectacular. Salmon opportunities are fewer due to the distance, and for the most part, limited in quality. You can fish for silvers at Moose Creek (mile marker 54.6), in late August and early September, but the run is only fair. As the Glenn continues its run west, there will be no more salmon opportunities until it runs through the town of Glennallen and into the Richardson Highway. Once you get there, you have a choice of direction. To your left, the fishing is fair. To your right, the fishing is good to excellent. The choice is obvious; turn right and head south towards Valdez.

You can fish for reds at the Klutina River (mile marker 101.1), from the last week in June through all of July. Fishing can be good to excellent. From there, you can continue south to the Little Tonsia River and Tonsia River Confluence (mile marker 74.5). Take the gravel road and bear to your right at the split. You will find fair to good activity for silvers near the end of September and the start of October. After that, there are no salmon opportunities until you just about reach Valdez.

Allison Point (mile marker 2.4 to 5.0), offers up excellent pink salmon

You have to see it to believe it. Salmon by the thousands can turn the the water almost black during peak runs.

fishing that peaks during the entire month of July. It also supports good fishing for silvers during the last weeks of August and the start of September. You will be casting from the shore directly into the bay. The Robe River (mile marker 1.5), also offers up good Silver salmon opportunities in mid September. A dirt road will lead you a half mile to a split where you then go about another half mile in either direction to find your spots. The highway also crosses this stream about another mile down the road before the pavement ends.

Pink salmon fishing in Valdez is phenomenal right from the shore. This is the place where I saw the water actually turn black because there were so many fish. There is an artificial fishery developed for pinks in Valdez, so that means you can catch them every calendar year. Valdez is the pink salmon capital of Alaska. You would have to see it to believe it. Pinks are there in the millions.

The Port of Valdez is in a majestic setting. There is so much ice and snow around there, that it sometimes is referred to as "Little Switzerland." Even during the peak of summer, the ice and snow remain. Look up. It is hard to fathom, but extreme snow skiers actually hold their annual competitions from those peaks. Part of the terrain that surrounds this community will take your breath away. Waterfalls on the highway system abound. Valdez is stunning.

The Glenn and Richardson highways are both beautiful areas in terms of scenery. I do not regret visiting them. But my purpose in guiding you is to put you on the fish in the most efficient manner. It is a long way back to Anchorage from Valdez, and it takes the greater part of a day just to return. For that reason, this highway system is ranked least in opportunity. My advice is to skip the Glenn and Richardson highways your first time out and return to them another time.

Pink salmon crowd up at Valdez.

THE GEORGE PARKS HIGHWAY

This is the moderately-used highway north of Anchorage that offers great fishing opportunities that are not too distant. Vehicle pressure is not heavy. You catch it by leaving Anchorage on Highway #1 to the north of the city. It runs about 35 miles until it splits to your left near the town of Wasilla, and becomes known as the George Parks Highway and Highway #3. This highway runs 358 miles all the way to Fairbanks and is a one-way run. Again, you will have to turn around and go back the way you came after you fish it.

I definitely would suggest roadside fishing for salmon from this highway, and I will support that rec-ommendation for some very good reasons. The first reason is that it is a relatively easy drive to the fish. You will not have to go far on this highway to find opportunity. Every roadside spot you could wish for will be found less than 150 miles from Anchorage. The second reason is that this system supports a variety of salmon. All five species are available from it, and the recommended target species of pinks, silvers, and reds can easily be reached by highway access. Chum salmon frequent this area, and pound-for-pound they are reason number three for you to be there. I really do not need yet another reason to convince you, but I will throw it in, anyhow. As you drive north on this highway look to your left and over

George Parks Highway

Salmon Fishing Forecast

Location	Species	Timing	Rating
Bird Creek	Pinks and Chums	July and August	Good to excellent
	Silvers	Late July and August	Excellent
Willow Creek and Susitna River Confluence	Pink and Chums	Mid-July to early August	Good to excellent
	Silvers	First few weeks of August	Good to excellent
Willow Creek	Pinks and Chums	mid-July to early August	Fair to good
	Silvers	first few weeks of August	Fair to good
Little Willow Creek	Pinks and Chums	July and August	Good
	Silvers	Mid August	Good
Caswell Creek and Susitna River Confluence	Pinks and Chums	July and August	Good
	Silvers	August	Excellent
Sheep Creek Slough and Susitna River Confluence	Pinks and Chums	July and August	Excellent
	Silvers	August	Excellent
Sheep Creek	Pinks and Chums	July and August	Good
	Silvers	August	Good
Goose Creek	Pinks and Chums	July and August	Fair to good
	Silvers	August	Fair to good
Montana Creek	Pinks and Chums	July and August	Excellent
	Silvers	August	Excellent
Sunshine Creek an Susitna River Confluence	Reds, Pinks, and Chums, Silvers	July and August August	Fair to excellent Good to excellent

20,000 feet of an added bonus will complement your drive. The tallest mountain in North America, Mt. McKinley, is part of your experience when you enter this highway. On clear days, you cannot miss it.

The easiest and most productive way to fish this highway is simply to drive north. This route parallels the Susitna River. Some spots are right at bridge crossings. Other spots require that you turn off the highway and drive down dirt roads and then hike in.

Any area noted as a confluence will be where the tributaries of two flowing waters meet. In this system, it will mean the streams of any given creek are emptying into the Susitna River. A confluence area offers superior opportunity in salmon fishing. There are always more fish where the two waters join.

Angling opportunities will begin at the Little Susitna River (mile mark-er 57). Pink and chum salmon fishing is good from mid July to early August, and silver salmon fishing is fair to good during the middle of August. This is a seldom crowded easy-access area just off the highway in a park setting.

Thirteen miles north is the Willow Creek and Susitna River confluence (mile marker 70.7). Drive into the campground and hike to the spot. Pink and chum salmon fishing is good to excellent from mid July into August. Silver salmon are available during the first three weeks of August, and are also rated the same. Always expect crowds at any fishery adjacent to a campground and a confluence area. The Willow Creek Bridge (mile marker 71.4), offers nearly duplicate opportunities in fish and timing, but the fish numbers will be less and so the rating decreases to a quality of fair to good.

The dog-tired author sits at a table stacked with freshly-caught salmon steaks.

Immediately north is Little Willow Creek (mile marker 74.7). Pinks and chums are there in July and August, and silvers peak there during mid August. Little Willow is a very picturesque and slow-moving stream with sandy banks and clear pools. I always enjoy exploring it. Pressure is light and fishing can be good.

About ten miles up the road is the Caswell Creek and Susitna River confluence (mile marker 84.1). Head a half mile down the dirt road and then hike down the bluff. There is good fishing for pinks and chums especially during July and August. Silvers can be taken during the month of August, and fishing for them can be excellent.

Sheep Creek Slough and the Susitna River Confluence (mile marker 85.8), comes next. You will have to drive about a mile and a half down a dirt road and then hike down an embankment to fish this spot. Fishing for pinks and chums is split between the months of July and August. Silvers are in during the month of August. It is a tight spot to fish, but fishing can be excellent. A heavy Pixee spoon works well here. Cast out as far as you can.

Continue north and and you will immediately cross Sheep Creek (mile marker 86). That is where I was bridge spotting with a friend. Get out and have a look and you will see what I mean. pinks, chums, and Silvers will be on the same time schedule as the Sheep Creek Slough. And once again, the quality of the runs will decrease a notch since you are away from the confluence area. This is a very easy place to fish. You can almost fish right from where you park your car.

Goose Creek (mile marker 92.7), offers up fair to good opportunity for pinks, chums, and silvers just like sheep. The better fishing will be found if you hike a mile to the confluence area once you cross the bridge. Just follow the flow of the stream to get there.

My most favorite fishery in all of this highway system is Montana Creek (mile marker 96.5). Montana has a terrific campground located adjacent to the water, and the areas of the campground and fishing streams are quite vast. You can even camp at the creek's edge in some spots. Montana's waters split into a variety of finger streams that are well worth probing, and eventually they all lead to the creek's mouth on the Susitna River. Fishing for salmon at Montana's confluence can be exceptional. The largest chums I ever fought came from the Montana, and it is a great spot to harvest pinks and chums during the July to August split. Silvers are there during the entire month of August. Expect to do some light to medium combat fishing at the confluence area.

The mountain-climbing town of Talkeetna is just over 15 miles away from Montana Creek and I advise you to go and visit it. This is the town that serves as the entrance to Denali National Park and offers all kind of visitor opportunities dependent upon your time and budget. You will enjoy this community.

If you still have salmon on the brain you can drive further north. The Sunshine Creek and Susitna River confluence (mile marker 102.5), can be found by driving a half mile on a dirt road and then hiking a short distance in. A fair run of reds is there during the split between July and August. Pinks and chums can be good to excellent at the same time. Silvers will be in during August with the same quality.

By now you should have found your fish. I have listed ten terrific spots for salmon. The George Parks Highway is worth every bit of your time. I rank it as having very good highway fishing opportunities. Beyond the information I have shared, though, there is yet another reason for you to be in this area. If you wish, you can elect to enter this system because it will be one of the most memorable drives you will ever experience in your life.

THE HATCHER PASS ROAD

Hatcher Pass is a crawling and winding 49 mile gravel and dirt road that connects the Glenn and George Parks highways. Its boundaries are located at mile marker 49.5 on the Glenn Highway, and at mile marker 71.2 on the George Parks Highway. You will actually be able to drive and cross a mountain range at elevations that will put you next to ice and snow if you elect to explore this road. A 271-acre state park that features a gold mine is along the way. It is a summer-only opportunity and is not recommended for large RVs or trailers.

Hatcher Pass will show you the origins of many rivers and streams. You will see water stage itself in development from thundering over boulders, to resting in placid beaver ponds. Views in the pass are staggering, and on a clear day you really can almost see forever. If the weather is clear and you have the time, I would strongly recommend that you enter the George Parks

Highway via this route and enjoy the adventure.

Pick up the Hatcher Pass Road just a little west of the community of Palmer off the Glenn Highway. When you complete the crossing, this journey will spit you out just north of the town of Willow on the George Parks Highway. If you take this route, you will wind up north of the starting point of the Little Susitna fishery. You can either pick it up on your way back, or you can turn south on the George Parks Highway and drive the seventeen miles to reach it and then head north. It is your option.

Consider Hatcher Pass dependent upon driving conditions and vehicle size. I would omit it on a rainy day. If the day is overcast or sunny, I would go. Seldom does a roadside opportunity give you so much for just the cost of your time. The drive is free; there is no fee. If you want tranquility on the way to the crowds, it awaits you there. You will not regret it.

As you can see, the reasons to drive north from Anchorage speak for themselves, so also will be the reasons to head south. The third and final highway system can be the most productive of them all. It is also the most crowded, and at times, the most congested. Join in! The southern routes are very much worth your time.

THE SEWARD AND STERLING HIGHWAYS

These are the two highways that offer up some excellent salmon fishing opportunities all over the place. Vehicle pressure on both of these highways can be heavy. You catch these highways by leaving Highway #1 to the south of Anchorage. One

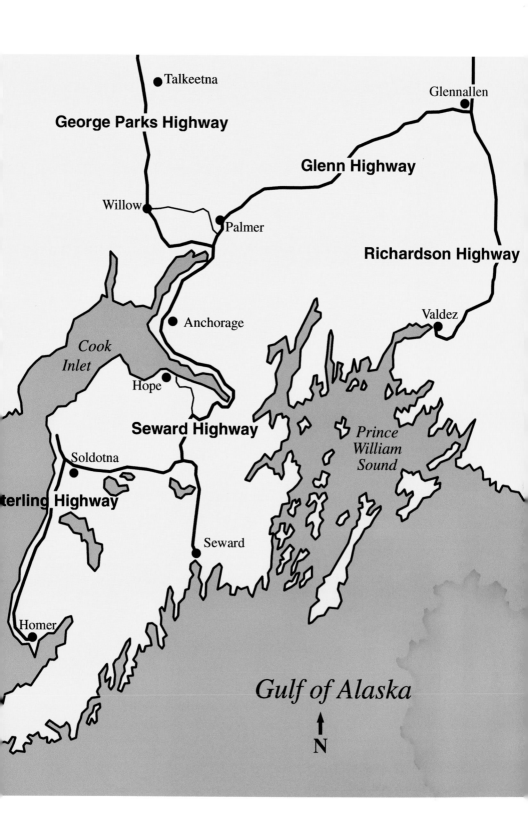

continues south and is known as the Seward Highway. It runs about 127 miles and continues all the way to the community of Seward. Once it passes the Sterling Highway cutoff, it changes to Highway #9, but it is still recognized as the Seward Highway.

The Sterling Highway is the other significantly larger half of this southern route. It remains Highway #1 all the way to its end. The cutoff is about 90 miles from Anchorage and from there it winds all the way down the Kenai Peninsula to the utterly charming seaside community of Homer. The distance from Anchorage to Homer is 233 miles.

Both of these highways are one-way runs. Once again, you will have to turn around on each in order to return

Seward and Sterling Highways

Salmon Fishing Forecast

Location	Species	Timing	Rating
Bird Creek	Pinks and Chums	July and August	Good to excellent
	Silvers	Late July and August	Excellent
California Creek and Glacier Creek Confluence	Pinks and Chums	Late July and early August	Fair to excellent
	Silvers	August	Fair to good
Six Mile Creek	Pinks and Chums	Late July	Excellent
	Silvers	August	Fair to good
Resurrection Creek	Pinks and Chums	Late July	Excellent
	Silvers	August	Fair to good
Seward Beaches	Silvers	Mid to late August	Good to excellent
Kenai River and Russian River Confluence	Reds	Mid-June and late July	Excellent
	Silvers	Mid-August and early Oct.	Fair to good
Kenai River	Reds	Mid-June and mid-July	Good to excellent
	Silvers	Mid-August and early Oct.	Fair to good
Moose River and Kenai River Confluence	Reds	Late June and mid-July	Good to excellent
	Pinks and Silvers	Mid-August to early Sept.	Good to excellent
Swift Water Park	Reds	June and July	Fair to excellent
	Pinks and Silvers	August and September	Good to excellent
Funny River and Kenai River Confluence	Pinks	August	Good
	Silvers	Mid-August and mid-Sept.	Good
Kenai Spur Highway	Reds and Pinks	Mid-July and early August	Good to excellent
	Silvers	Early August and	Good to excellent
Crooked Creek	Silvers	Early September Late August and Early September	Fair to good
Crooked Creek and Kasilof River Confluence	Reds	Early to mid-July	Fair
	Silvers	Mid-August to early Sept.	Fair to good
Ninilchick River	Reds and Pinks	Mid-July	Fair to good
	Silvers	Mid-August	Fair to good
Deep Creek	Pinks	Mid-July to early August	Fair to good
	Silvers	Mid-August	Fair to good
Starski Creek	Pinks	Mid-July to early-August	Fair
	Silvers	Late August to early Sept.	Fair
Anchor River	Pinks	Late July and early August	Excellent
	Silvers	Late August to early Sept.	Good
Homer Fishing Hole	Silvers	Late July and September	Excellent

to Anchorage. Both highways meander through valleys and coastal plains, offering tremendous views of mountains and glaciers. Both support ample camping grounds and roadside motels. Most importantly, both offer some excellent roadside opportunities for the first time economy angler.

THE SEWARD HIGHWAY

As soon as you leave Anchorage, the Seward Highway begins by running parallel with the edge of an immense saltwater fjord. Captain Cook sailed those waters over 300 years ago looking for an inland passage. He failed. The fjord ended, he had to turn around, and so he adeptly named it Turnagain Arm. Unlike the historical Captain Cook, you will not fail. One of Seward Highway's most popular and successful salmon fisheries is at mile marker number 101.2 and is recommended by me as your first stop. This fishery is known as Bird Creek.

Bird supports an ample population of pinks, chums, and silvers. Pinks start in July and peak toward the the last two weeks of that month. Fishing for them can be good to excellent. Chums start in July, and are rated good to catch until almost the end of August. Silvers start during early July, and peak during the month of August. This gives them an excellent rating. Bird is a tidal creek. It is influenced by the rise of the sea, with salmon flooding into it at high tide. This creek is an excellent place to start your southern route. It is also an excellent place to begin to learn how to fish for salmon if you have not done so before. Many times I start my fisheries there. Camping opportunities are directly adjacent to this area.

You will be in moderate to heavy combat fishing at the Bird. Move around and follow the flow of the fish as they rush in. This is a very productive fishery and limits can be taken there. Fish are not the only stars at Bird Creek. So are the fishermen. As you fish the waters below, look up to see the tourists above. Tour operators

Bird Creek is so easy to fish the whole family will enjoy it.

bring them in by the busloads to allow people a chance to see a fishery operating at full steam. Now you are the star. Enjoy your moment.

Bird Creek is one of my favorite spots. If there ever was a fishery that best illustrated the flows of the tide and the importance of timing, this is the one. You will discover glacial silt at Bird, and you will soon recognize the importance of shifting your feet as you stand and fish. If you do not move about, the incoming flow of shifting sand can literally lock you into place and you will be stuck. Bird is where my tackle box floated away, and as you fish this area, you will understand why. You can learn much from Bird that will be applicable to some of your other roadside fishing locations. It is a top-notch fishery if your timing is right. It is also a top-notch place to learn how to fish for salmon. Those are two very good reasons for spending time at Bird.

As you continue to drive south, the California Creek and Glacier Creek confluence (mile marker 89.8), awaits you if you hike a quarter of a mile upstream and fish just beyond the railway bridge. Pink and chum salmon are there during the July and August split. Pink fishing can be excellent, but chums are only fair. Silvers are strongest during August with fair to good results.

Salmon opportunities lessen as you wind your way down the Seward Highway. Although the streams are there, there is no hope for decent salmon runs in them. You are, by far, better off to head for Hope itself.

THE HOPE CONNECTION

At mile marker 56.1 on the Seward Highway, there is a paved cutoff that runs 17.7 miles to the tiny town of Hope. The road is a one-way run, and like almost every road in Alaska, once you get there, you will have to turn around and return the way you came. The Hope Highway offers up three salmon species.

Sixmile Creek (mile markers 7.1 and 8.5), will have short dirt roads that lead to even shorter hikes for some quality fishing. Fishing for pink salmon and chums can be excellent near the end of July. Silver salmon

Wildflowers grace the road's edge in Hope.

are rated fair to good during the month of August. Once you leave that location, you can drive to the end of the highway, and you will wind up in town at Resurrection Creek (mile marker 16.3). Pinks here are rated excellent towards the end of July, and chums come on just as strong during that same period of time. Silvers filter in during August, and are also fair to good opportunities.

This fishery is among the most scenic in all of Alaska. Resurrection Creek splits into fingers as its mouth empties, and many smaller streams occur that fill with fish. The fishing distance, from the creek to Turnagain Arm, is lengthy and unobstructed, and its scenic background is complemented by snow-covered mountains. The stream is crystal clear, easy to walk and wade, and no more than thigh deep anywhere. Combine that with the sound of rushing water and the calling of seagulls, and you could have just about the most picture perfect spot you could ever wish for. If that was not enough, throw in the dusty main street of an old gold mining town that is so small you can idle by all the buildings in less than a minute. If you can imagine all this, that is Hope.

Needless to say, Resurrection Creek is among my favorite spots. It is out of the way and seldom are there many people. On a sunny day, I will schedule my entire itinerary so that I can do a picnic lunch there. There is not a lot of old Alaska left around on the highway system that you can visit by car. Hope is an exception. Hope is historical. If you are heading south and can fit this one in, do it.

Once you return to the Seward Highway, there will not be any more roadside salmon opportunities until you just about reach the community of Seward itself. Seward means Silvers. If it is August, you are heading in the right direction.

THE COMMUNITY OF SEWARD

Seward is the southern terminus of Highway #9. Though you have run out of highway, you certainly have not run out of roadside opportunity. At the peak of the salmon run, the harbor in Seward fills with sea-bright silvers. They are fresh, ferocious, and all over the place. So too, are the tourists. The town can be alive with fishermen, and the Silver Salmon Derby will be in full swing. Seward is an extremely busy town once the silvers arrive. Plan and reserve ahead.

You have to fish for silvers directly from the beaches around Seward because there is no freshwater fishing for salmon permitted beyond that opportunity. Make sure you do your research so that you time your arrival to coincide with that of the fish. Here's a tip to help you. The website of the Department of Fish and Game has its own search engine. Type in "salmon archives" and you will find the data you need. They even have a phone number you can call for weekly reports. Up-to-the-minute information is critical here. Peak opportunity can occur at any time from mid to late August. If the fish have hit the beaches and you are there, it couldn't be more perfect for good silver fishing. If they are not there, then you have a problem. You can either pay your way out of it, or move on.

Seward is full of charter opportunities. They will take you to the silvers for sure, but you will have to pay for it. I cannot endorse this if you are looking to save money. But you are in Alaska, and Seward is located on the Kenai Fjords, and they are absolutely breathtaking to appreciate from a boat. Tourists pay good money just to cruise these fjords and look around. A fisherman gets the same views tossed in for free when he pays to fish. If it was sunny, or overcast, and I was there and the fish were not, I would pay. It's really up to you.

Seward is an interesting coastal community. Punch it up on the web and you will see that there is plenty to do around the area, including a visit to an aquarium with indigenous Alaskan marine life. I booked a charter once when I was there, and I still don't regret it. I can vividly recall being in a glassy cove surrounded by towering snowcapped peaks. It was a bright summer day and glaciers were calving, every

time they broke, it sounded like distant cannon fire. All this took place as I reeled in my limits of salmon. It was worth every penny.

If you do elect to move on, there is now only one highway left for the first-time angler, and that is the one that the whole world uses. Welcome to the Kenai, and the end of the road.

THE STERLING HIGHWAY

As mentioned, this highway starts as a cutoff from the Seward Highway, 90 miles outside of Anchorage, south on Highway 1. At the cutoff it remains Highway 1, and continues all the way down to Homer. This 143-mile length is known as the Sterling Highway. Fish migrate to the northern half of this peninsula via one single great river, the Kenai. Migrations at the southern half come directly from Cook Inlet. This highway supports a tremendous amount of roadside opportunity. The two favorite targeted salmon, reds and

Sometimes there is an added bonus when you go out charter fishing; note the Tanner crabs.

silvers, are both major players from this highway. Some of the best roadside fishing in all of Alaska takes place here. As a result, the Sterling can at times be extremely busy. Drive with care.

As soon as you take the cutoff, start counting the mile posts. All the action starts about fifteen miles down the road. The big river you soon will see is the Kenai, and you cannot miss it. The first major roadside location is the Russian River Campground (mile marker 52.7). This site is undoubtedly the most popular highway fishery in all of Alaska. This area is where the confluence of the Kenai and Russian rivers meet. Its fishing quali-

ty is legendary. More salmon swim by a highway angler here than any other spot on Earth.

Sockeye salmon are the stars of this fishery. They will be there two times in two separate and distinct runs. The first occurs around mid June. The second occurs around the last week of July. Both runs last about two to three weeks. Both runs are excellent. Expect combat fishing conditions to be as heavy as you could ever experience in your life. Fishermen at the confluence area can at times be almost shoulder to shoulder by the hundreds!

Silver salmon also play a role at this fishery, and they also run twice.

Get in, have fun, and get out again without your pocketbook taking a beating!

*Angler Evan Duke shows that catching sockeye salmon
can take place in an area of incredible beauty.*

*A combat fishing zone on the Kenai River is worked
hard during the second run of red salmon.*

They start to arrive around mid August and then return later during the first week of October. The first run can be good fishing. The second will be fair. Both runs last several weeks. All of this makes for an extremely busy fishery, but to the informed highway angler it just represents another outstanding opportunity. It really is one of the greatest highway fishing spots you could ever imagine, and it's yours for the taking.

Once you secure your parking spot at the Russian River Campground, you will have to hike to the confluence area. The campground is large, and the walk is via the trail that parallels the Russian River. Follow the flow of your fellow fishermen to the right as they walk the Russian downstream for about a half hour to the confluence.

Although I speak about your attire and equipment in later sections, it is very appropriate to first mention it here. The only thing you should carry into this fishery is your equipment and backpack. The walk in is downhill and easy. The walk out is uphill and strenuous. If you have caught your limit of fish, you could be returning with up to 30 pounds of salmon.

For that reason, I recommend taking a good-sized backpack. Carrying fresh-caught fish by hand that far, and uphill, will wear you out. Heft them on your shoulders in your pack and the return trip will be easier. It is the sensible thing to do. If you camp at the Russian you will have to do this, you have no choice. It is the price you pay for one of the most premier highway fisheries in all of Alaska. And don't forget, take your time as you walk out.

The *Milepost* will show other fishing areas that you can hike to while at the campground. Those fishermen who turn left and walk upstream on the Russian will avoid crowds and can search out opportunities along the river. It is all a matter of timing and choice.

Things are upside down at the top of the world during midsummer. The sun hangs low in the sky for a long time. It does not set until well after midnight. Crowds let up when people go home, then the fishing pressure decreases. Take advantage of this circumstance. You can fish for salmon in adequate light at 10 p.m. in this area. I told you Alaska was a matter of timing. In this circumstance, fishing late gets you a better spot.

After you leave the campground, there are more opportunities down the road. These areas will continue to present themselves for the next 125 miles.

The Kenai-Russian River Ferry (mile marker 55), can get you to the confluence if you are not camping. You will have to pay a fee to park, plus a fee to ride the ferry. This convenience is excellent, but crowded. The Kenai is so powerful that the current is actually harnessed to literally drag the ferry and its occupants across

A "river hottie" graces the view on the Kenai River.

The author fishing at 9:30 p.m. in the Alaskan twilight.

the river. You will wait in line, and then be packed in like a sardine. When you get to shore you then have to seek out your spot in the combat zone. Do not lose your ticket. You will need it for the return trip.

One of my most memorable experiences occurred right in this crowded lot. As I ferried back from the confluence, I ran into a fisherman who was carrying an entire platter of cooked fish. He had run out of streamer flies and was trading freshly prepared red salmon steaks for terminal gear. I reached into my vest and gave him three new flies. He pulled out a paper plate and gave me three terrific steaks. I was hungry. He was in need. It was a fun swap and we both laughed as we did it. The spirit of Alaska can be just as flavorful as what I ate that day. It is my hope that

you will savor that taste throughout your entire trip.

As you drive south, the Kenai River offers up several more spots via the pullouts and trails between mile markers 55 and 58. Reds will be there during mid June and mid July, and fishing for them can be good to excellent. The silvers will be there around mid August and the start of October in fair to good numbers. Both species can run for two to three weeks. If you wish to get off the highway, you can do it at Skilak Lake Road (mile marker 58). You will find a number of access areas and hiking trails within a five-mile stretch that will lead you to the Kenai with the same exact fishing conditions but less crowds. This road rejoins the Sterling Highway just past mile marker 75.

The Kenai will continue as a major player the farther south you go. The Moose River and Kenai River Confluence (mile marker 82.3), sees a fair run of reds the last two weeks of June, and a good to excellent run of reds starting in mid July. Our good friend the pink, shows up the first two weeks of August in excellent numbers. Silvers are good at mid August, and again at the start of September.

The next highway fishery is located near the municipality of Soldotna at Swift Water Park (mile marker 94.1). Soldotna itself is just a mile down the road. The Kenai flows directly through the heart of this town, and the fishing industry is built upon it. There are privately owned motels and campgrounds in Soldotna that have excellent bank-fishing opportunities if you are paying to stay with them. There are also free day-use municipal parks that offer fishing opportunities. Ask around. Lots of people will be at Soldotna when the fish are in, so expect moderately-sized crowds particularly in the free areas. The Kenai is a big and swift and cold river. Reds are in it during June and July; silvers during August and September. Pinks scurry about during almost all of August. I seldom pick Soldotna as a destination to fish due to the immenseness of the river and the commercialization of the area. Whether or not you choose to do so is a matter of personal choice.

The Funny River and Kenai River confluence (mile marker 96.1), can be reached by driving about twelve miles down the Funny River Road. Park your vehicle, cut through the campground, and hike to the spot. Pinks are good during August. The first run of silvers will offer up good fishing starting the second week of August, and last for about a month. The second run is also good. It starts in mid-September and will last about three weeks.

As you leave Soldotna, there is a 40-mile one-way highway known as the Kenai Spur that is to your right. It offers your last roadside chance to fish the Kenai River near where it

Wild beauty runs right down to the shoreline on Cook Inlet.

empties into Cook Inlet. Tides will play a big factor in the flow of fish, so make sure you pick up a free tide chart at any tackle retailer before you leave town. Although the Spur runs for miles, you need not go the distance. Mile marker 5.1 has a road that runs about a half mile to the river. Mile marker 6.4 has a road that runs about three miles to the river. And mile marker 10.5 has a road that is just about a mile in length to reach your spot. Salmon opportunities in all three areas will be the same. The late run of reds can be good to excellent the last two weeks of July. Pinks will vary in strength as July ends and August continues. Silvers will be your best bet. Both runs last several weeks and can be good to excellent from the start of August and again starting mid September. If you have opted for this fishery, turn around and head back to the Sterling Highway after you have finished.

DOWN THE
KENAI PENINSULA

Most fishermen simply continue south from Soldotna on Highway 1. At this point, there are about 50 miles of the Sterling Highway left until the end of the road. All the roadside waters will flow directly into Cook Inlet and that tidal card now becomes even more important to have. Although the fishing quality loses its excellence somewhere along the way, it picks up near the end. There are still plenty of opportunities and interesting things to see.

Crooked Creek (mile marker 110.9), will offer up one run of silver salmon that starts during the split between August and September and lasts a few weeks. Fishing for them

can be fair to good. But you are better off to fish the Crooked Creek and Kasilof River confluence (mile marker 114.5), just beyond the Crooked Creek Campground. Red salmon fishing can be fair during the first three weeks of July. Silvers can be fair to good starting the last two weeks of August and into the first week of September.

The next two fisheries are located almost on top of each another. They are just two miles apart. Ninilchick River (mile marker 135), can have fair fishing for reds during the middle of July. Pinks are good to excellent during the July and August split. Fishing for silvers can range from fair to good for several weeks beginning in mid August.

A charming Russian Orthodox community known as Ninilchick Village is located at this river. It is unique to all Alaska. Take a break and walk around and enjoy the culture you will discover. America purchased the entire territory of Alaska from Russia for less than two cents an acre in 1867. Most Russian heritage has long since disappeared, but in Ninilchick, it survives.

Deep Creek (mile marker 137), has an access road that runs a mile until you reach where it empties into Cook Inlet. Pink and silver opportunities should be similar to the Ninilchick, but reds will not be around. Always be attentive when you are in a tidal creek area. By now you are probably glad that you took the time to experience it way back at Bird Creek.

Starski Creek (mile marker 151), serves up some pinks during the July and August split. Silvers are offered the last week of August into the first two weeks of September. Fishing for both is only rated fair. From there, there is only one more river left as you head south.

The Anchor River (mile marker 157), is the last freshwater river left on the highway system. As you drive down the Anchor River Beach Road a mile and a half on the way to your spot, congratulate yourself. You are now at the most westerly point on the North American continent accessible by road. If you arrive there during the adjoining weeks of July and August, you will find fishing for pinks to be almost excellent. Silvers will run the Anchor River during the last weeks of August and into the first week of September. Fishing for them should be good.

You have just about reached the terminus of the Sterling Highway. As a matter of fact, there are only about 20 miles more of it until it ends. The only thing left is one more community, and one more unusual and spectacular roadside opportunity. Welcome to Homer and the end of the road.

THE HOMER SPIT

As you have been driving the highways, you have by now learned that they spit you out here and there among the mile markers. In Homer, the meaning of spit changes completely. It is used to identify the unique setting of the community itself. The Homer Spit is a slender slice of land that juts five miles out into Kachemak Bay, and on it rests the entire fishing industry. Your highway leads you to it, and this elevated view of where you are heading presents itself to you before you arrive. For some, this picturesque setting alone is worth the drive.

Homer is known as the halibut capital of the world. Almost all activity in this town is centered around that opportunity. Fishing for halibut is arranged by paying for a charter. It is a very productive and costly proposition. Although I have not led you to Homer for that, it is certainly worth addressing later in this section. For now, let us return to salmon and tides because, when

The seaside shops in Homer are utterly charming.

combined, they lead to a worthwhile and unique salmon fishery.

THE FISHING HOLE

The second-strongest tidal bores on Earth are in Cook Inlet and include Homer. The drop between high and low tide can range from 20 to 30 feet. Recognizing this, and realizing the predictable change, the state of Alaska took advantage of it. Not long ago, engineers dug a massive hole the size of a small lake in the center of the spit. They then dug a single trench from the hole to the bay. When the tide is high, water fills the trench and becomes a small stream that empties water into the hole which has since become a small lake. When the tide is low, water empties out and the stream disappears. Since the lake has been dug so deep that it never completely empties, whatever swims into it at high tide is captured and remains in the hole. Think of this setting as a gigantic flush toilet where nothing overflows or goes down the drain and you will be able to visualize this concept.

After the excavation was completed, biologists from the Department of Fish and Game released salmon fingerlings into the lake. The hope was that at the start of low tide they would flush out and return to sea. It was further hoped that years later, as adult salmon, they would sniff out their origins and return to the same spot. This experiment worked. The returns were unbelievably successful.

The fishing hole now supports adult populations of king and silver salmon. A good-to-excellent run of kings arrives by the end of May, and drops into the hole for about four weeks. A second fair-to-good run of kings returns in mid July, and drops in for another four weeks. Silvers flow into the hole in good to excellent numbers just about all of August and September. This entire fishery is artificial and is absolutely designed for the highway angler. It ranks among the easiest of any opportunity you will ever meet in Alaska. All you do is park and fish. It should go without saying that this type of accomplishment is extremely popular. The fishing hole is open seven days a week and never closes. There is no fee to fish it. Expect crowds at this location, especially at high tide. Once again, you will be combat fishing. By now you should be an expert.

Although I have not endorsed fishing for kings your first time out, if you ever wanted the least expensive and most reasonable chance of landing one, here it is. Your only requirements are stout tackle and the purchase of a king salmon stamp. Good luck to you.

THE ACE IN THE HOLE

I would hope that by now the information I have given you has allowed you not only to target your salmon, but to catch them as well. If for some reason you have been unsuccessful, Homer is where you can consider spending a little extra money to make you happy. You can pay your way to a victory harvest by fishing for halibut. These brutes go all the way from 25-pound chickens to 100-pound barn doors. Even larger fish are caught and landed. Size is just a matter of luck between who holds the rod and the size of the halibut that bites it.

A charter will supply you with all instruction, equipment, bait, a licensed skipper, and about ten hours of fishing opportunity. There are no guarantees, but rarely does any paying client return to the dock without reaching the limit of two halibut. And just like in Seward, the views alone are worth the price. Marine mammals will complement your trip along the way. The chance to view otters and whales is the norm on almost any Homer halibut charter. If you need to play your ace in the game of fishing, play it here.

If you fish by day, you will be dog-tired by night, and Homer is a great place to stay. Opportunities to spend the night are abundant. Researching those opportunities can lead to some memorable discoveries. The last time I was there, the accommodations I rented included the full use of my host's garden. I was invited to pick fresh greens and vegetables to accompany the evening dinner of grilled halibut steaks and salmon sushi appetizer. Everything I ate that night was harvested by me. It was the freshest, most rewarding meal I have ever had while on the road.

Daytime activities in Homer abound. There is a museum and a marine refuge that both attest to the wildlife and sea that surrounds them. There is also a 20-mile scenic drive that starts above the community and drops right down to it. There are driftwood beaches and beached relics. There are shops and restaurants and plenty of temptations. You will never find a more charming seaside community in all of Alaska than Homer. What's on the end of this road simply could not be nicer. Enjoy it.

MOVING ON

Now that you know when and where the fish are, it is time to discover the information that can get at them. The next two sections deal with that. You need a place to stay, and a way to get around. Everything will be centered on when you arrive and when you will be departing. It is time to pull out your calendar and put together your checklist. You will soon be on your way.

A halibut catch that displays what happens when you play your ace in the game of fishing.

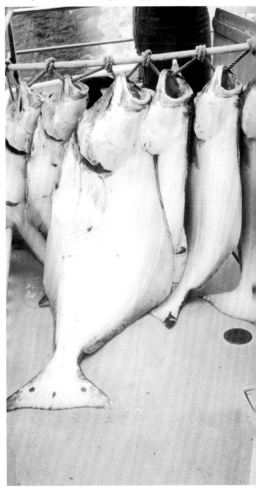

This 52-pound halibut isn't even worth Alaskan bragging rights, but it sure ate well!

 # Chapter 6

Arranging Your Flight and Itinerary

Since you have determined the best time to fish, it is appropriate to look carefully at your flight options. You will remember that I advised you to put time on your side, and that I urged you to book as early as possible so you would not lose any flight opportunities. When you start checking around with the carriers, you are probably going to find that airfares are very similar among most of them from your destination to Anchorage during the summer. Price probably will not be a factor in determining your carrier.

If you have enrolled in a credit card mileage program, and are flying on a voucher, your carrier is already picked. You probably will have very little choice as to the time of your arrival or the time of your departure. Some things are just carved in stone. But if you do have options in selecting your carrier, be sure and examine their arrival and departure times. These times can vary and are critical to your itinerary.

By the way, since you have booked early, you can request the most convenient and comfortable seats. There are not a lot of options in coach, but there are some spots that I consider to be better than others. I always request as far forward an aisle seat as I can get. This is for convenience. Aisle seats offer more room, but no view. I also ask for exit row seating once I am at the airport. Exit row seats will give you a little more leg room.

Since you have been ticketed so many months ahead, be aware that schedule changes in your original ticket can occur. It is best that you call your carrier every couple of months to keep up with these changes. They are usually minimal changes in flight number or arrival and departure times. Certainly you should take the time to call and double-check everything a few weeks before you depart.

The timing of your flights is critical. Chances are you and your party will be moving several checked items per person. Give yourself plenty of time by arriving at the airport well ahead of departure. This is especially true if you are checking a weapon in your equipment. Make certain that you clearly understand what your responsibilities are, and follow instructions to the letter. No margin of error is tolerated concerning a firearm, ever.

I check as much of my luggage and equipment that is permitted, and then carry on-board a shoulder-strapped, insulated vinyl cooler. If you scout around at a large sporting goods store, you can find one with several compartments. The ride to Anchorage is long, and you cannot count on airline food to satisfy a hungry traveler. This cooler will prove to be invaluable not only on the plane, but in your rental vehicle as well.

ARRIVING IN ANCHORAGE BY DAY

If you are arriving in Anchorage during regular business hours, you couldn't be off to an easier start. Your vehicle rental facility will be open, and all you have to do is pick up your mode of transportation, and away you go. It could not be more simple. If you can book a flight that gets you into Anchorage during the day that allows for this simplicity, definitely do so.

Unfortunately, things do not always work out that way. Depending upon your city of origin, and the airline connections out of it, you could wind up in Anchorage after regular business hours. This could have a major effect on the start of your trip, especially if you are renting a large recreational vehicle and your dealer is not open. Arrangements made to personally accommodate you when a dealer is closed can be costly, and with some dealers is prohibited. The only way you will know what option is available, is to check ahead via research. Avoid any recreational dealer who is insensitive to your needs.

ARRIVING IN ANCHORAGE BY NIGHT

A lot of flights arrive in Anchorage during early to mid evening. When you arrive at that time, you are either going directly to your rental vehicle or to a motel. I have mentioned before that motels in Anchorage during peak summer are expensive. I do not recommend spending the night in Anchorage whenever it can be avoided. You are much better off to plan a trip that allows you to immediately leave Anchorage once your flight has arrived. Besides, chances are good that on your return trip home, you will have to stay in Anchorage anyhow prior to your leaving.

If you do arrive in Anchorage at night, after you pick up your rental vehicle, be sure and inquire from your rental agent for the major stores open 24 hours. This will give you a chance to stock up on fresh food that you couldn't bring in, or to purchase items that were not available in your departing location. Fishing licenses and salmon fishing equipment will be included in those stores. Recreational rental vehicles of massive size will fill their parking lots at night, and these parking areas transform to become urban blacktop campgrounds. Get your things and move on.

The Chugach Mountains offer up a spectacular view right outside of Anchorage.

Driving in the dark is okay, but not for the first-timer just starting out. I recommend that any late-arriving highway angler should consult the *Milepost* and rest in one of the many roadside turnoffs or parks outside of Anchorage and wait for first light. This will give you a chance to rest up from all the frenzy of your travel day. You have no doubt traveled far. Plus you have had to go through the responsibility of securing your rental vehicle. And you have just finished doing a major shop in a strange store you have never been to before. Chances are good that it has taken you considerable time to get to where you now are, and you have undoubtedly crossed several time zones. You are on the top of the world. Rest before you start your journey.

Arranging the route of your fishery is completely up to you. At this point, you are bound to make choices based on the run of the fish and the run of your time. Put the two together, and there is your trip. Some accommodations can be found by leaving it up to chance, while others will have to be reserved. It is all dependent upon where and when you go. Running the highway routes becomes an option based upon how much time you have out in the field.

THE SINGLE-HIGHWAY TRIP

This trip is the easiest to plan. You pick one highway system and you fish it. After you are done, you turn around and head back to Anchorage the way you came. The Seward Highway and Sterling Highway are both good examples of the one-highway option. So also would be the George Parks Highway. Even the lonely Glenn or Richardson highways are worth your attention. Your decision is all a matter of where the fish are and the time you have.

A single-highway trip is advised for those fisheries where you have anywhere between four to seven vacation days. Certainly you could spend more time on a single highway if you wished. It is your option.

THE DOUBLE-HIGHWAY TRIP

This trip is a little more sophisticated to plan. You pick two highway systems and fish them both. After you are done, you turn around and head back to Anchorage from the last highway. Combining the Sterling Highway, with a run part way down the Kenai Peninsula, and then flipping around and crossing through Anchorage to fish the George Parks Highway is a classic example of the double-highway trip. Once again, it is a matter of where the fish are and how much time you have.

The double-highway trip is advised for those fishermen who have a total of nine vacation days or more. You can reach both of these systems if you have a minimum of seven full days in the bush. I usually split the week in two, and plan to cross into Anchorage during regular business hours. This affords me the opportunity of stopping in at a fish processor to either hold my dressed catch in a freezer, or to have my iced whole fish smoke-processed and later shipped home.

Although I speak specifically about what to do with your catch in another section, it is relevant to say that on a double-highway trip you are going to need to do something with your catch before you change locations. Crossing in Anchorage allows for this. And speaking of Anchorage, it is now relevant to explain how this city figures into your trip.

THINKING AHEAD

Regardless of which highway trip you pick, be aware that by the end of your journey you are going to be tired and dirty. By the time you head for Anchorage you will probably have coolers full of fish, dirty waders, and soiled clothing. Your rental vehicle will be littered with fishing gear, road maps, bedding, and whatever else you picked up down the road. In short, you will be a mess. The last thing you want to do is face a lengthy return home under these conditions.

Give yourself a night in Anchorage before you fly home. This will allow you to take care of all those responsibilities that are detailed in my final section. Research your motels and find one that offers freezer space. This is imperative if you are checking fish home. If it has laundry facilities, that is an added bonus that you will use. Many flights leave for the lower 48 states early to late in the evening from Anchorage. They are called red-eye flights and are the norm in order to make city connections the following morning.

You cannot leave this part of your itinerary to chance. You must reserve in Anchorage ahead of time or you will pay dearly for what rooms there are, if any. Although you could score a cheaper room outside the city, I do not recommend it. Leave nothing to chance on your return home. Besides, Anchorage is an enjoyable city. In all probability, once you overnight, you will have some free time to kill, and Anchorage has plenty of opportunity. The tour book I advised you to get

from an auto club is your best helper here.

After you lock in your final night, return to your maps and resources to examine your chosen route. You are soon to be a highway angler. You will fish by day and sleep by night. You are going to need a place to stay, be it campground or motel. You do not have to reserve every night, and in fact I encourage you to deliberately structure part of your trip on the fly, so that you have the flexibility and opportunity to chase fish dependent upon where they are. Opportunity like that abounds on all three highway systems. Just keep some general things in mind.

CAMPGROUNDS

Campgrounds usually have plenty of opportunity to reserve from mid morning until mid afternoon. After late afternoon, some can fill fast. This is generally true of most state public-use campgrounds. Just be sure to keep in mind that when you are driving to a location to put yourself on fish, you will be joined by others. Alaska has plenty of campgrounds. If you cannot find a spot where you hoped, another may be nearby.

Some of the private-use campgrounds will not have this opportunity due to the return of favored customers. Private-use owners cater to the client by offering such perks as free firewood, hot showers, freezers, laundry, and private bank-fishing opportunities. They are also in premier locations, and some people stay there for months. If you are seeking one of those campgrounds, make reservations months ahead of time. As always, there are exceptions to the rule. Sometimes a phone call is an easy way to check for availability.

MOTELS

The same circumstances that confront a camper will also confront the highway angler who prefers to stay in a motel. There are usually openings from mid morning until mid afternoon. After late afternoon, most motels hang the "no vacancy" sign. Once again, it all depends on where the motel is located relative to where the fish are. If the fishing is hot, so will be the pressure on the motel. If it's not, the equation reverses itself.

Most motels will not let you check in until mid afternoon, and many expect you to check out before noon the following day. The nice thing about securing a motel reservation on the fly in the morning, is that you can fish your heart out the rest of the day and not worry about where you are going to stay. Seldom would I endorse looking for a motel in late afternoon or early evening. By that time you have waited too long and you will probably be out of luck.

PRESSURE AREAS

There are some areas that would be senseless to try to fish without reservations. When the silvers are forecast to hit the beaches in Seward, adjacent campgrounds and motels are booked solid. When the Red Army is forecast to be at the confluence of the Russian and Kenai rivers, adjacent campgrounds and motels fill up. These are two classic examples. So it would go in the community of Homer at the peak of the Halibut Derby. So also is it at Anchor Point during their Silver Salmon Derby. In some areas, you must reserve. Your research will indicate those places to you. In such circumstances, I strongly recommend that you reserve ahead of time.

Pressure areas can be rewarding; they attract highway fishermen for good reason. That is where the fish are. If you are on your way to any location and you encounter vehicles parked everywhere, and fishermen carrying fish, then stop. There is no better indicator of quality fishing than that. Crowds can be valuable if you keep an open mind and look upon them as an opportunity. Conversations are quick to come when people are happy and catching fish. Talking with those who are walking out can provide you with immediate information as you prepare to walk in. All it takes is a complement and a friendly smile. Seldom will any fisherman not treat you like one of his own. All you have to do is ask.

DOWN THE ROAD

Arranging your itinerary is one thing. What you drive on the roadways is another. Rental vehicles in Alaska run the gamut from compact cars to fully-equipped motor homes over 30 feet long. Before you hit the road, pick out exactly what you are going to drive down it.

Roadside encounters with moose will usually encompass both cow and calf.

Chapter 7
SELECTING YOUR RENTAL VEHICLE

The rental vehicle business in Anchorage is a big business. There are agencies in and around Anchorage that rent cars, trucks, sport utility vehicles, vans, custom vans, truck campers, and motor homes from 20 to 30 feet long. These agencies have packages that in addition to the rental itself, can include bedding, sleeping bags, coolers, propane stoves, folding chairs, outdoor grills, housekeeping packages, and other items all the way down to a chemical toilet and the biodegradable paper that you use with it. In short, the options are endless.

Researching these opportunities is equally as varied. Agencies will advertise in magazines, newspapers, tour books, and via brochures that usually come in any Chamber of commerce request you make. Also, you can use a keyword search on your computer and another whole world of information will come motoring out at you. Type in "Alaska RV rentals" and you will see what I mean. The last time I did that I stopped counting the websites after I reached 200. That is what I mean by big business. You will not have a difficult time finding information in this area. There is plenty of it.

All the highway systems I have pointed out to you will accommodate any of these vehicles. All the salmon fishing locations, equally noted, will allow you to park these vehicles nearby. You need not worry about getting stuck, or hav-

ing to rent a four-wheel-drive vehicle, so long as you remain on highway paths and are careful when you turn off them. Operating all of these vehicles is mainly just a matter of common sense and good judgment. Be not afraid; instead, be informed.

What you decide to rent will be determined by a variety of factors. These include the number in your party, the conveniences you desire while on the road, whether or not you choose to stay in a park or a motel, and most importantly, cost. All of these factors are personal, and are the ones you'll have to consider in order to find what is best suited to your needs.

It is little wonder that I have advised you to plan ahead. Once you get your information and ultimately make your decision, you will have to make reservations. Vehicle rental opportunities in Anchorage are just like Anchorage's motels. Competition during peak season is high. Prices are high. You must reserve ahead of time or you won't have many options. Reserving "ahead of time" means making your commiting six months before you plan to arrive.

SMALLER VEHICLES

The smaller vehicles are the easiest. They operate much like the traditional automobiles you use at home. Cars, trucks, SUVs, vans, custom vans, and truck campers are included in this category. They go anywhere, and will also park anywhere. They are ideal for one person, or two, and perhaps even three. Once you reach a party of four or more, you will have to move up in size.

If you are staying overnight in motels, your vehicle need only be adequate enough to allow for the size of your passengers and their supporting luggage and equipment.

In a later section I speak more specifically about personal gear, but for now it's important to recognize that each first-timer will be advised to come to Alaska with one cooler, one soft-sided suitcase or duffel, and perhaps one rod case. Always include these items as you plan. They can fill even a full-sized four-door car in a hurry. Think carefully about what you are bringing into Anchorage, and select a vehicle that will store what you have checked.

If you are camping, then your vehicle choice needs to be the truck camper or custom van designed with sleeping space for passengers. Two persons are ideal in this type of set-up. Even three can make it in a squeeze play if you are organized

An angler repacks a custom van at a campground spot.

and determined. And speaking of organized, take a look at what I do.

Remember my dedication to custom vans on page 2? I usually rent a custom beauty van in Anchorage for my party of two or three. My host picks me up at the airport no matter what time I arrive. He then transports me to his business location, where we finish all our paperwork, throw in our rented sleeping bags and camper package, and we are off. Each night all we have to do is press a button and a full-sized bed rises forward from the rear of the van. If there are just two of us, we just pull down the shades inside the van and we are asleep. If there are three of us, the third folds both the captain's chairs down flat, and once that bed is made, that passenger is asleep, too. It could not be more simple or efficient.

Even a small tent could be added to make sleeping arrangements a little more comfortable for the small vehicle camper. Many summer nights in these are wonderful for a tent outside. If it rains, you can always squeeze back into the truck or van. If it does not, you get to sleep under the stars. Believe me, the stars up there are closer than anywhere else on Earth. It is little wonder that more people elect to camp out in the Last Frontier than stay in a motel. Spend just one night out in the open and you will understand what I mean.

LARGER VEHICLES

The larger vehicles are more complicated. Due to their length and height, greater understanding and respect must be undertaken when using them. They operate somewhat similar to your automobiles at home, but due to their size, more care must be exercised during their operation. Motor homes are included in this category. They go just about anywhere, but parking them is a different manner. They are ideal for a party of four or more, and some of the larger motor homes will comfortably accommodate an adult party of up to six persons or more.

The motor home is designed exclusively for the park camper. These homes on wheels are engineered to be totally self-sufficient. Many have their own holding tanks for water, a generator for electrical power, propane for cooking, and even a shower. They have ample storage areas for all your needs inside the home, and just as ample cargo areas for all your storage needs below the home. All the appointments in a motor home will be there right down to the video player, television, compact disc stereo, and the fully-equipped kitchen with a stove and refrigerator. In short, they are engineering marvels.

Private campgrounds cater exclusively to these homes. Many parking spots are designed so that the arriving camper need only hook up to a power and water source, and the motor home has perpetual utilities without even running a generator. Even if a hook-up is unavailable, so long as there is gas in the engine, there is power.

The larger the motor home, the larger the responsibility. It should go without saying this also means the larger the price. But do your math. You might find that once you split costs, it becomes individually affordable. Many dealers require that you go through an hour or so check out before they release these homes to you. All will recommend that you use a spotter in your party to get out and assist you each time you park. All leasing agencies require heavy security deposits, and all have contracts with a lot of fine print. Read this information carefully before you make your decision. Share this information with your automotive insurance agent; you will not be charged for this service anyhow, it is free. Let your insurance professional guide you to the right decision concerning your liability and your responsibility. A good motor home can provide you with many Alaskan memories that will cause you to smile.

The largest motor home I have ever come across was at Montana Creek north off the George Parks Highway. It had been rented by a large group of men from a Norwegian family. Included in the family were younger teens, fathers, cousins, uncles, and even the older grandfather with a great flowing and majestic beard. "Every year," the Scandinavian patriarch told me, "we work like idiots so that we can afford to come to this place to fish. We fish back home, but nothing in Norway is fantastic like Alaska. We could not be happier here than anyplace in all our lives." As I looked around and saw family members involved in different stages of cutting, filleting, packaging, cooking and canning salmon, I realized they were not idiots at all. They had converted their motor home into a custom fish processing factory on wheels. As the two of us sat next to the embers of his evening fire, I sipped the homemade brandy-fla-

vored coffee my new friend had offered me. When I heard the howl of a distant wolf, and looked up to a full and silver-bright Alaskan moon, I realized I was just as happy as he was.

ADDED FEES

Agencies add fees in a variety of ways, and this is especially true with motor homes. The only thing you can do is research your options and then come to a decision about what you consider is a fair deal. Face it, you will not have room to check sleeping bags and cooking equipment on your way to Alaska. You will have to rent them. And if you leave your motor home extremely messy, you will have to pay for that, too. Leasing agencies already have your deposit, you must play the rental game by their rules or you will pay even further out the nose. Just be sure to read the rules and then abide by them.

Some agencies charge you by the mile. Others have a daily quota of free miles then charge you for additional miles. And others offer unlimited miles for free the entire length of the lease. These factors will influence your decision. Remember what I said about the highway systems. They are not vast, and you, as an economy angler, need not travel far. That is why you have a road map and a section that dealt with an itinerary before you got to this one. Now that you know where you are going, simply add up the total miles and use that sum to help you make your decision.

All agencies offer the added insurance option no matter what size the vehicle. Again, make sure you consult with your own auto agent as to what you should do. Any lease agency should be willing to send you a blank contact ahead of time for you to do this. If not, avoid them. Your taking the time to do this is smart business. The adage of "an ounce of prevention is worth a pound of cure" is more than fitting when you are behind the wheel of a vehicle worth well over $50,000. Please follow this advice.

THE ANCHORAGE RENTAL

Since I have advised you to build an itinerary that includes a return and stay in Anchorage the evening before you depart, you should consider your transportation needs while in the city. Certainly you will no longer need a motor home or any other larger vehicle. And certainly you would not want to drive it around in congested urban traffic. I save considerable money by

When the top bud blossums on this Fireweed, it will signal the end of summer and the approach of fall.

scheduling to return my primary rental vehicle towards the end of the day as I return to Anchorage. I then immediately rent a smaller and less expensive vehicle from the airport for that evening, and use it the rest of the following day.

This method allows me to cruise Anchorage in comfort before I leave. I can park anywhere with no worry. Usually all my baggage is locked in the trunk by the following day.

Even a larger party can rent a passenger van in this manner. Not only is this a cost-saving move, it does wonders for convenience. When it is time to catch your flight home, all you need do is top off the tank, return the vehicle to the airport, and your responsibility is finished.

Do your research and look at your schedule. This may fit right in. If it does, make your second reservation.

DISCOUNTS

Do not forget what I mentioned earlier. If you book early, you sometimes can get a discount on your rental, but this is more applicable to larger-sized vehicles. Even if an early discount is not advertised, it may still be available. Agencies are sometimes receptive to a planner who is willing to make a fiscal commitment more than a half year ahead of the game. All you have to do is ask. You might get lucky.

THE FISH ARE CALLING

Enough of all this technical advice. It's time to get down to the most exciting part, the fishing. What you need to harvest salmon is called equipment, and much of what is required you probably already own. The next section deals specifically with what you need to catch and land salmon.

Chapter 8
CHOOSING YOUR EQUIPMENT

When you walk through the doors of any sports merchandiser anywhere, you will see more equipment than you can believe. The choice of materials that confronts you seems almost endless. There are aisles of rods, and racks of poles. There are counters of reels, and shelves of tackle boxes. Row after row of terminal will hang like ornaments on a holiday tree. There are waders and vests, and hats and sunglasses. Custom clothing and raingear hangs around just like the nets and the knives that will tempt you. If you do not know what you are looking for, and turn yourself loose, your pocketbook is going to take a serious beating.

The advice I am about to give is not meant to alienate the conservationist or the fishing purist who advocates catch-and-release. These fishermen contribute to deserving and respectable roles in helping to maintain the world's natural stocks of wild fish, and I commend them for what they do. In fact, at times, I am even one of them. But when I roadside fish in Alaska for targeted species that are in great abundance, I exit their ranks and cease to be a member of that fraternity. Instead, I fish hard with stout tackle in crowded conditions. I take my daily limits. I do this in order to bring home a most delectable prize that I thoroughly enjoy.

The flat rod case can serve to store both rods and reels if you check it on the plane.

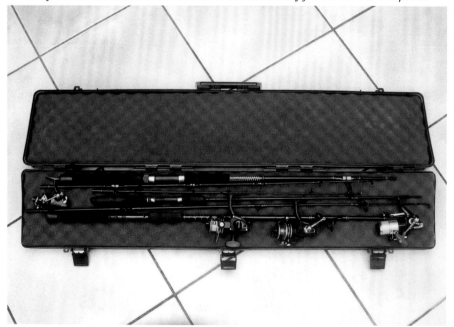

The expectations in a crowded roadside bank fishery are relatively simple. You will need to fish with equipment designed to present your lure or bait in an efficient manner to enable the fish to strike. Once this happens, this same equipment must enable you to bring the salmon quickly and immediately to shore. You will have little room to play it, due to both current and adjoining fishermen. Your fish will arrive untired and full of life. You will then either net it or drag it onto the shore. It will arrive flipping and flopping, and you are then required to stun it into submission. This whole scenario is commonly called "horsing in your fish". It is my observation that the most adequate and effective equipment to use under these circumstances is a spinning rod and an open-faced spinning reel. They are the least expensive and most dependent systems to get this job done.

Rods

The majority of fishing locations I have noted require a medium- to medium-heavy-weight spin-fishing rod. A break-apart rod, ranging from six to seven feet in length will accomplish the rest. If it is low-budget and cheap fiberglass, it may break. If it is mid budget and a combination of graphite and fiberglass, it will probably hold up. If it is high-budget and solely graphite in composition, it will be superior. This type of rod can handle sockeye, coho, and chum salmon effectively. Bring two of them.

I also use a lightweight spinning rod that breaks apart and is about six feet in length. It will be mid budget in cost and I use it to fish exclusively for pinks. Bring only one.

In addition, I carry a reserve spinning rod at all times (in my backpack). Most of these are telescopic and low budget. Some are multi-break-apart and mid budget in cost. This rod is your ace-in-the-hole in case your primary rod breaks while fishing. Try to find a medium-weight rod about six to seven feet in length. Bring only one.

A rod case can be used to pack these four items. It will be counted as checked baggage. Find the most generously-sized case you can so that you can pack additional support gear in it. In the event your carrier limits your checked baggage to two items and a carry on, omit the case and simply bundle your rods together and carry them on board.

Reels

Those same fishing locations mostly require medium- to medium-heavy open-faced spinning reels. Match the reels with the rods. Buy an additional spool for each reel. This is advised so that in any given moment you are prepared to replace or switch out line if you need it. Quality reels will handle your targeted species effectively. Bring two reels in this category.

You also need to have an open-faced spinning reel that matches your lightweight spinning rod that you'll use for pinks. Match your reel with your rod. Buy an additional spool for the reel. Select a quality reel. Bring one reel in this category.

In addition to the reserve rod that you now carry in your backpack, add in a reserve reel. Match it to the rod. The reel should be medium weight. Carry this with you at all times. Buy an additional spool for this reel. This reel is your ace in the

The Little Cleo is the favorite of many anglers throughout salmon country.

The Steelie is an inexpensive medium-weight wobbler and is used by many anglers throughout salmon country.

Unweighted wobblers of medium to large size can be cast with dropper leads utilizing three-way swivels. They work well for kings and silvers

The Pixee is a weighted wobbler available in several sizes and colors. The larger sizes are perfect for salmon, especially kings and cohos. Because of their weight they work near the bottom and that is probably one of the reasons they are so effective.

Drift bobbers are very popular and productive with or without bait. The Spin-n-Glo, and Corky, as well as the Glo-Bug are easily found in tackle stores.

Additional Alaska Tackle Suggestions (Frank Amato)

Flatfish diving plug.

Banana-type plugs which dive
and wiggle, such as the Flatfish,
Tadpolly, WiggleWart, and
Quickfish, can be cast and
worked from shore by using a
light dropper weight of hol-
low pencil lead on a sep-
arate piece of leader
connected to a three-
way swivel. They are easy
to lose in snaggy water so use
them in sandy-bottomed, or peb-
bled sections of stream. Kings
(chinooks) and silvers (cohos)
especially like their action.

Wiggle Wart diving plug.

*The Blue Fox weight-
ed spinner is a big
favorite wherever
salmon are found.*

*Many anglers prefer to make their own
weighted spinners to get exactly what
they want and save a bit of money, too.*

**Additional Alaska Tackle Suggestions
(Frank Amato)**

hole in case your primary reel breaks while fishing. Bring one reel in this category.

If your rod case is generous enough, you may be able to fit these four reels in it. That is why I recommend a large case. You will spend hours casting and retrieving, and during hook-ups your reels will be subjected to lightning-fast runs. Inexpensive reels simply do not hold up to the constant pressure they will be subjected to when you fish for salmon in Alaska. I strongly advise that your reels be mid budget or better. Avoid cheap equipment and you will never sit frustrated on the banks of a premier fishery like I did so many years ago.

LINES

If you have been following my advice, you now realize that you are going to have up to eight spools that you have to fill with line. I strongly advise you take those spools to your favorite fishing store and have them professionally filled and labeled on the inside of the spool. You will not pay that much more, and what it does for casting and switching out will be appreciated by you.

All line that I use is ultra-limp monofilament. It casts very well and is reasonably priced. I admit that there are some delightful new high-tech braided lines out there, but they are more expensive. Line, though, is a matter of personal choice.

Two of the spools on the medium- to medium-heavy reels should be filled with 17-pound-test line. The other two extra spools should be filled with 20-pound-test line. If you are going to ignore my advice and fish for kings, buy yet another spool and fill it with 25-pound-test.

The two spools on the light-weight spinning rod that you are using for pinks should have 8-pound-test line and 12-pound-test. The two spools that are using for your reserve reel in the backpack should be spooled at 17- and 20-pound-test lines.

Now that all the lines are spooled, go back and buy individual packs of the same test lines for each spool so that you can replace them all. A salmon on the run can burn out a spool in a matter of minutes. As a first-timer, you can expect to make some mistakes as you fight these fish. And by the way, I have not told you yet, but a foul-hooked salmon stuck in the back or in the tail runs like a freight train. Replacing and replenishing fishing line is the norm up there. Be prepared by being supplied.

FATAL ATTRACTIONS

The remaining items required to fish Alaska's salmon are swivels, lead, hooks, spoons, flies, and even bait. All of these items are known collectively as terminal gear. If I sent you back to your favorite sportfishing merchandiser, I am certain that I would find you back there in that same aisle of those hanging ornaments wondering what to do. The choices for terminal gear are staggering. Here is what you do. Count one, two, three, those numbers represent the choices you are going to attach to the end of your line. You are going to tie on either a spoon, fly, or hook.

The spoon you are advised to use is a ball-peened silver or gold-colored spoon called a Pixee. It comes with a colored plastic insert and a single-treble hook. Preferred weights are 1/2 or 7/8 of an ounce. They are deadly, and I am of the opinion they are Alaska's most used lure. They are available at all the fishing stores in Alaska and also via mail-order catalogs such as Cabela's, Bass Pro, and L.L. Bean.

The fly to use is the Russian River Streamer Fly. It comes with a long shank wrapped with colored deer hair. It is very specific in size and is manufactured to conform to the regulations of Alaska's Department of Fish and Game for its use in the confluence area of the Kenai and Russian rivers for reds. It is equally as deadly in all other locations, and in my opinion, is the most-used fly in all of Alaska. Its availability is the same as the Pixee.

The hook you are advised to use is the standard single-barb salmon hook. It ranges in length from 1 1/2 to 2 inches long. The width from the point of the barb to the shank is about 1/2 to 3/4 quarters of an inch. It is used in conjunction with either fresh or processed salmon egg segments that are wrapped on the hook with a piece of fine meshing. It is very effective in locations that will permit you to use bait. Buy your bait and hook presentations at stores in Alaska. Any clerk will gladly assist you if you take the time to ask.

Those three major terminals are all that you will need. They fill my cooler each and every trip. Bear in mind that the longer you fish, the more support terminal you'll use up. Spoons snag. Flies bounce and get caught. Hooks tangle up. Fish break lines. I arm myself with spoons, flies and hooks by the dozens. The last thing you would ever want to experience is to be caught short in the field because you have run out of terminal gear. Plan ahead.

The only other items left are swivels and lead. The swivels come in two types, both barrel and snap on. Barrel swivels are used to make leaders, and snap-on swivels can be used to attach spoons. These items should be sturdy enough for strong fighting fish. A medium length swivel from a 1/2 to 3/4 of an inch will suffice fine. Have plenty with you.

Leads must range in assortment due to currents. You can use split-shot, egg, crimp-on, or pencil. You will use weights ranging from 1/8 of an ounce to a 1 ounce depending upon where you are and what terminal you are casting. I seldom pack lead. Instead, I buy it in Alaska. Be certain that you have a generous amount. Ask your Alaskan clerk to demonstrate how to use pencil lead if it is new to you. It is more expensive and requires a special swivel set up, but it is very convenient because you can cut it to meet your needs.

WHAT ABOUT YOU

Everything I have recommended deals with what you need to actually catch fish. Nothing has been mentioned concerning what you will personally need when you are out there fishing for them. Just as the Norwegians converted their motor home into a mobile fish-processing factory, so will I convert you into a completely mobile fisherman. In the following section, I explain how this can be done so that you can face all the elements without a care in the world.

 # Chapter 9

NECESSITIES IN THE FIELD

After the highway angler gets off the road and out of the vehicle, the sole destination is the river or stream. Some of these locations are short walks on well-worn trails that require a pleasant stroll that only takes minutes. Others are not so easy. Reaching your location can sometimes encompass hikes over broken trails that can take as much as a half to three quarters of an hour. These jaunts can be on level or steep terrain. It all depends on where you wind up. Every fishing spot is different in the degree of difficulty to reach it. Some are easy, some are not.

Once the spot is reached, the angler is faced with accessing it. Investigate the general area to determine the optimum location for you to fish. Along the way, you might have to traverse steams, climb steps, and walk over logs. Eventually you will make up your mind where to stage yourself when you find the space that best provides for your needs. Once you locate it, you may be there for hours. This is the routine for those who fish from all of Alaska's highway systems.

As you remain there, you are out in the open and "in the field". You are subject to whatever climatic conditions Alaska prefers to throw your way. You will have sunshine and clouds, and you will have wind and rain. None of these elements should deter you if you are properly dressed. Remain steadfast and focused, and you will continue to cast and catch regardless of what the heavens bring

down upon you.

As you fish, your lines will snap and terminals will be lost. You will rig leaders, tie on swivels, and replace lures. Fish will be landed, and fish will be lost. If you are in a tidal area, you will shift and move and go with the flow of the water as you follow the flow of the fish. If you are escaping the crowds, you will be hiking even longer and further to get away.

In short, you are forever on the move. The last thing you want is to have to return to your vehicle because you have forgotten something. Be prepared. Equip yourself to be completely mobile and protected while you are on the move. Nothing should encumber you, and everything you carry and wear should have a purpose. From head to toe,

A good backpack, wide brimmed hat, amber glasses, and personalized jacket leaves little doubt as to where you are heading

you need to be ready. From head to toe, here is what you need.

Hat

A broad-brimmed hat serves a great function in Alaska. The forward bill keeps the glare of the sun out of your eyes, and the side and rear brim allows water to drain off onto your shoulders. If you are in a buggy area, it keeps those pests out of your hair. A hat is essential. Select one that is water-resistant.

SUNGLASSES

There are two types that you need in Alaska. One is the polarized version that allows you to see into the water by removing glare. Be careful as you shop for sunglasses, they can get quite expensive. A budget-priced pair with coated plastic lens works adequately. Coated glass is even better, but is more expensive.

The other glasses I heartily recommend are "shooter's glasses". These are the ones with bright amber or yellow lenses. You have no idea how much they can brighten up a dreary day until you put a pair on. You will find them in the hunting department at your sports store.

TACKLE BOX

Forget about anything hard sided. Select one that is soft sided so that you can pack it in your suitcase or duffel. You will not even carry it to the stream. It should be left behind in your vehicle. I will never forget how utterly dumb I felt when the incoming tide washed away my tackle box at Bird Creek. One minute it was on a rock, the next minute it was gone. That was the last hard-sided tackle box I ever bought.

FISHING VEST

Your vest is your mobile tackle box. It goes wherever you go, and it never gets washed away. Everything you need in terminal gear for a whole day's worth of fishing can be stored in your vest. If you are not used to owning one, you soon will be. A vest is imperative. A budget-priced vest is fine providing you take care of it.

When my wife and I are on the rivers and streams of Alaska you cannot miss us. Both our vests reflect the region we come from. I stopped into a sewing store one day, and found some great embroidered and sequin decals that I asked my wife to sew on the back of each of our vests. Her vest now has palm trees on the back. My vest has flamingos on the back. This little personal touch has led to many opening and friendly conversations with complete strangers.

And now a note of caution. If you know you are fishing swift waters, a vest that is a combination flotation device is a wise investment. Most areas I pointed out to you will not require a flotation device, but any area that has depth and current is treacherous if you slip and fall in. A flotation fishing vest could save your life. Please give this recommendation some extended thought.

RAIN GEAR

It will rain on you in Alaska. A quality rain outfit is a necessity. Most outfits come in coat-and-pant combinations and are priced separately. Avoid the bottom line in price. In a rain outfit, you get what you pay for. Breathable fabric that is water repellent is excellent. You will find a vast array of choices via mail-order catalogues from those big three suppliers

I mentioned to you in the last section. Matter of fact, everything I am recommending, from head to toe, can come out of those catalogues.

BACKPACK

This an extremely important item. You will rely upon your pack in the field all of the time. You will put everything in it, and at times this will even include your fish. Select a pack that is roomy and has some outside pockets. Make sure the shoulder straps are foam insulated so that they will not cut into your shoulders when the pack is heavy. Look for a pack that has exterior tie straps. The straps will enable you to tie on your waders if you do not want to wear them as you walk.

Avoid budget-priced backpacks. Just like with your rain gear, you get what you pay for in a backpack. The straps on my pack allow me to hang it on a tree and I do that all the time to keep it off the mud and sand. If I have to set it down, I just whip out a plastic garbage bag from the rear compartment, and wrap it around the pack with a twist tie. A wet and soiled pack is a nasty item to have to store in your vehicle. Thinking ahead prevents this.

WADERS

There are two types of waders to use in Alaska. There are those that come to your hips, and there are those that come to your chest. Most river and stream fishermen I observe use hip waders, yet there are others who wear chest waders. All of the areas I have pointed out to you can be fished by either wader type. Selecting your wader style is up to you.

I enjoy using hip waders because they increase my mobility. They are easy to walk in due to the absence of a seat and chest area. Plus, you can even fold the tops part way down when you hike, and that promotes an even easier walk. Hip waders allow you to fish water as deep as your thighs, and in swift current you should be no deeper than that anywhere. The only drawback is that if you hit an unknown hole as you wade, hip waders fill with water in a matter of seconds. When that happens, you are out of the picture until you dry off.

Chest waders protect you from getting wet all the way to chest-high level. Some anglers prefer this comfort, and that is why they wear them. If you do select this type of wader, I suggest the neoprene design that hugs the chest tightly. In the event you do fall, this design would prevent water from rushing in.

Regardless of what type of wader you select, make sure you purchase a repair kit that matches the wader's composite material. Stick this tiny kit in your backpack and carry it with you at all times. Always rinse your waders, and never leave them in the hot sun. Take care of them and they will take care of you.

FIRST-AID KIT

A small kit is always recommended when you are in the field. You just never know when an injury is going to happen. You can buy one or you can make one, but either way, it belongs in one of the compartments in your backpack.

ON YOUR BELT

A good fillet knife is essential to the highway angler. You can count on cutting your catch now that you are following my advice. You will need at least a medium-sizde blade and also a large-sized blade. I always bring two. One hangs on my waist at all times. I have already told you how I use it for kings. Bring a small stone to hone your edges and store that in your vehicle. Dull blades are useless.

Needlenose pliers need to hang on your belt as well. The very first salmon you land will have the tip of the barb shoved up the shank and it will be deeply embedded in the flesh of the fish. The pliers are a must to work the hook out. They also become used in the game of catch-and-release that I will explain to you later in the section on Technique and Etiquette.

MISCELLANEOUS MUSTS

A stringer is essential. Zip that one in your vest. Leave the heavy metal one behind and stick with plastic which is lightweight.

If you field dress your salmon into fillets, you are going to need gallon-sized zip-lock freezer bags. Store the bags in your vehicle, but carry some in your back pack. If your intent is to simply gut your salmon and leave it whole, make sure you have a stout bristle brush to remove the blood that is packed all around the spine. Tie the brush on your backpack.

Heavy-strength plastic garbage sacks with twist ties are invaluable. Carry some in your pack at all times. They can wrap your fish, your clothes, your muddy shoes, your pack, and even your toes if your waders spring a leak. Sometimes I think those bags were invented for the highway angler.

Put together an emergency repair kit for your rods and reels. Mine contains a hot glue stick, a butane lighter, and an assortment of rod tips. I carry extra bail springs for every reel, lubricating oil, and a small multi-use folding utility tool. Since replacement equipment is always in my pack, I get to leave this kit in the vehicle to use if I need to make a repair of primary equipment at a later time.

Your last necessity may be your landing net. I used to carry one, but found that it annoyed me due to its cumbersome size. It wound up being yet another thing to carry and pack, and I seldom could fit it into my luggage or duffel. I used to buy a cheap net when I arrived in Anchorage, and then just hung it on a tree for some lucky angler to find when my fishery was done. If you are without a net streamside, there will usually be someone who has one nearby. All you have to do is be polite and ask, and it is usually yours to use for free. Most times, I simply bank land my fish. A net is your call.

GOT YOU COVERED

There you go, from head to toe I have thought of everything. There is even room in your backpack for a light lunch and a change of clothes if you happen to slip. And if you packed in the can of soda, you were smart. It is now cold and waiting under the rock in the stream where you hid it. Crush the can when you finish, and use the empty zip-lock bag from your lunch to pack it out.

As you hang around these great places, you may meet some friends who live there year round who either fly or walk on four legs as they forage about. I will talk about both, and the weather that surrounds all of you, in the next section.

A laska is full of surprises. No matter how much research you do, and regardless of how well you have planned, expect the unexpected. Elements beyond your control can confront you at any time. A bug-free zone can become a bug zone. An outdoor area filled with people can suddenly be joined by a bear. A sunny morning can become a wet and rainy afternoon. This is the norm. Things will change.

The responsibility of any roadside fisherman is to recognize and understand how these changes play a role in any fishery. When the Boy Scouts of America initiated the motto of "be prepared", they probably had little idea

how this simple phrase could influence so many people. Let those two watchwords become yours. Being prepared concerns your comfort while in the field. Being informed equally concerns your safety. Both go hand in hand.

None of these elements, which are beyond your control, should interfere with your trip. As a matter of fact, you may not even confront any of them if you're lucky. I have done highway fisheries where I been out in the field a full week without a single mosquito, a sniff of a bear, or even a drop of rain. Unfortunately, this is not the norm. Those three elements are indeed up there, and you could meet one, two, or all three in combination

The remarkable taste of fresh-caught salmon is enjoyed by just about everyone and everything.

your first time up. The highway angler who is prepared will be ready for all of them.

BUGS

Alaskan's love to poke fun at their bugs, and the number-one insect they joke about is the mosquito. If you walk down Fifth Street in Anchorage shoping for souvenirs before the flight home, you will find dozens of stores that offer merchandise that are testimonials to where you have been. Included in those stores will be racks of t-shirts, and included on those shirts will be mosquitos. The mosquito has become one of the marketing stars of the Last Frontier, and for good reason. This pesky insect is part of the Alaskan experience, and it will not go away.

Surprisingly, it will not be as bad as you might think. Mosquitos are thick in tundra regions. They are profuse in areas bordering stillwaters, such as lakes. And they are also more prevalent in the interior of the state as compared to the coast. Two thirds of the destinations I have so far recommended, are exempt from these categories. I admit to mosquitos being around, particularly on the Glenn and Richardson highways, but overall, they are not a problem. You are apt to meet them more in your campground than on the stream. Technology will help you deal with them, there are products that exist which will help keep you in total comfort.

DEET

Deet is the most powerful anti-bug solvent you can buy. It comes in a variety of pump sprays and creams, and will absolutely prevent you from being bitten. However, Deet is a powerful toxin. Keep it out of your eyes

and off your lips, and as you use it make sure you wipe your hands dry from the film that it leaves on your palms. When you purchase this product read all the instructions carefully and follow them to the letter. A small vial of this repellent always belongs in your fishing vest. Never forget to carry it with you.

ANTI-BUG MESH

Catalogue suppliers also offer a full range of anti-bug garments you can wear over your clothing. Once you are zipped or snapped in, nothing can get at you. The only item I have ever purchased was a full head cover that was very inexpensive and compact to pack. I zipped that item into my fishing vest years ago. I have yet to unzip it and pull it out. I have never used it. If you are going where I am sending you, chances are you won't either. Garment meshing is needed only if you are fishing in those areas where mosquitos traditionally like to hang out. Purchase anti-bug mesh at your discretion.

CITRONELLA

This product is designed so that when it ignites, it produces a smoke that will keep mosquitos at bay. The aroma is usually lemon scented and not unpleasant. Citronella is available in a pressed sawdust coil, or in wax as a candle. You will find it in catalogues and at stores in Anchorage as you stock up. Perhaps you might want to consider it. If not, your campfire will suffice to help keep bugs at bay. Smoke deters bugs. That is one of the reasons you will find campfires going every evening when you stay in a campground. A campfire is a valued friend to any visitor.

The worst bug bites I have ever encountered were not mine, but my

My good friend and fine artist, Thomas Krause, does a remarkable job of showing us all who's Alaska's number-one fisherman.

wife's. The two of us were fishing a small lake off Glenn Highway, and, as noted, that road system is more centered to Alaska's interior than other roads. It was a beautiful, very sunny day, and both of us were fishing at opposite ends of the lake. When we returned to the van, I casually remarked that it seemed apparent she was again snacking on chocolate, because the melted drippings were caked all over her cheeks and elbows due to the bright Alaskan sun. It was not until she admitted to me that she had forgotten her repellent that I realized those drips were her own caked-on blood. A nasty black fly had gotten hold of her and had wailed the daylights out of her in minutes. Bug cream does little good if it's left in your vehicle and not on you when you need it.

One of the items I pack in my first-aid kit is a bite stick. It is about the size of a large fountain pen, and it contains a mixture of ingredients that will soothe any itch or bite. I recommend you purchase one, you will be glad you have it in the event you need it. You are now prepared to do battle with any forager in Alaska that flies. But this will not be the case with the other Alaskan forager who walks on all fours and weighs close to 1,000 pounds. That occasional highway angler you'll want to avoid completely.

BEARS

As you were looking through the racks of t-shirts back at Fifth Street in Anchorage, you undoubtedly saw images of another Alaskan star. You may not have seen him on your first trip up, but believe me, he is out there. Alaska is bear country. Any fishery location that I have targeted could be visited by a bear at any

time. Any other location that you wind up in can be visited by a bear as well. It does not make any difference whether you are in a campground, on a trail, in a stream, or even jogging in the park in the city limits of Anchorage. A bear encounter can occur anywhere. Being informed is your best protection in dealing with bears. And again, it's time for you to do a little homework.

Go back to your computer and type in the keywords "bear facts". When you do, you will discover that, once again, Alaska's Department of Fish and Game will provide you with plenty of free information. Request a brochure or browse the site. Either way, you will find plenty of facts and plenty of advice. Study this information and become familiar with it. Follow all the rules to the letter. The best defense against bears is being well informed, period. There is no other way to put it.

BEAR BASICS

The rules concerning you and bears are relatively simple. Do not surprise them. Do not crowd them. And, do not, under any circumstances, feed them. When you are on a trail, make plenty of noise. Let them know that you are around. If you see one, immediately back off and give it plenty of space. Keep food odors to a minimum, and leave no food out. If all this fails, and the bear elects to encounter you, hold your ground and never run. If contact is made, drop to the ground and curl up in a ball with your hands clasped around the back of your neck and play dead until the bear leaves.

None of this information is presented to alarm you, they are just the simple facts. Alaska is bear territory, learn what you are expected to know and keep safe. And speaking of facts, consider this one. The common domestic dog kills more people in Alaska than bears do. Bear attacks that result in human fatalities are rare. If you have followed my advice and are reading the *Anchorage Daily News* online, you will find tragedy sometimes surrounds outdoor activities in that region. The more you read, the more you will discover that very little misfortune comes from bear attacks on anglers.

It was during my first trip up to Anchorage that I saw my first bear in the wild. It was a black bear mother and her two cubs. As I was approaching the Russian River, and my trail reached the water's edge, she was approaching on the opposite side. As a result, the two of us met at the very same time and the only thing that separated us was a band of flowing water about two feet deep and 20 yards wide. As soon as she saw me, she turned and directed her cubs back into the woods. As soon as I saw her, I turned and directed myself to the trail downstream to give her more space. In reality, neither of us wanted to have anything to do with each other, so we both walked away. So it should always be with you when you are in the field. And talk about the unexpected, I had been in Alaska only 14 hours when that meeting took place. You never know when an encounter will happen, you only know that it might.

The Department of Fish and Game will post notices at many locations where bears have been spotted. You cannot miss them. They will let you know what has been around and when. And they serve notice so you stay informed and be prepared. Whenever I walk into an area with my friends, we always rehearse what each of our responsibilities would be in the event of a bear encounter. Additionally, I seldom walk a deep trail alone. I wait until a stranger shows up, and then the two of us walk in together. You will discover this happens frequently at some of those locations that require longer hikes. Total strangers become mutual friends when they practice bear strategy. Consider that a nice by-product of your Alaskan experience.

You can arm yourself with weapons against bears, but I do not endorse it for any first-timer. If you insist, that is your right and your option, but it is your responsibility to be knowledgeable in firearm usage if you elect to do so. Bear in mind that a rifle or shotgun will be an additional piece of checked baggage. Unless you can fit it in the case with your rods, you may have four checked pieces based on the gear I recommend you to bring. When that happens, you will have to pay the airlines more money, both ways, to check the additional item. You can check a handgun inside your luggage, but it will not give you much defense against a bear. You can also purchase an aerosol pepper spray in Anchorage. This can be used to deter bears, but it is costly. I suggest that you leave a weapon out of your economy trip to Alaska. Arm yourself with information instead. Knowledge will not cost you a dime.

Bugs and bears are not big problems. The third element is the one you are certain to meet, and one you cannot possibly overcome.

RAIN SHOWERS

"Any day in Alaska is a good day. Any day it does not rain in Alaska is a great day. And any day the sun shines in Alaska is an outstanding day!" I so firmly believe in those three statements, that I put quotations around what I just said. I am forever repeating those sentences to myself and friends every time I go up there. Those words relate to the conditions that will surround you every time you go. You can almost count on it.

Rain will not deter a determined highway angler. As previously mentioned, salmon continue their migratory journeys regardless of atmospheric conditions. You can catch salmon in the sun, you can catch salmon during cloudy conditions, and you can catch salmon during the rain. So long as you are equipped and attired, ready to meet them, they are yours. The key to dealing with the weather in Alaska is to dress in layers. Fronts come in, and fronts go out, day after day. Rain can move in fast in the Great Land, or it can stall and linger around. Your responsibility, therefore, is to be prepared to meet the weather regardless of temperature or moisture. Layered clothing allows you to do this by adding or subtracting apparel whenever it is needed. Layered dressing is the norm at the top of the world.

WHAT IS NEEDED

In addition to your raingear, your daily apparel should include a lightweight jacket, a sweater, a shirt, and long pants. Forget about shorts unless your pack has room to include a second set of bottom articles. Toss in a cheap pair of cotton gloves and a neckerchief as well. I always seem to find space for an extra pair of pants, underwear, and socks every time I venture out into the field. There have been times I have been drenched and was glad that I brought them along. A premier fishery can be ruined if you get cold and wet. A change of clothes is yet another ace if you need to play it.

Remember what I said about avoiding cheap rain gear? I learned that one the hard way on one of my earlier trips to Montana Creek. I had purchased an economy vinyl rain suit that was folded neatly into a little plastic pouch. Before the rains came, I opened my pack, unfolded the rain suit, and put it on. I thought I was fine. When the heavens opened up, the rain was accompanied by a 20-mile-an-hour wind that came out of nowhere. During that same instant, a chum salmon, whose weight matched the wind speed, struck my line. As he rose completely out of the water, I could see the barb of my Pixee stuck firmly in his back. He went on a nightmare run. I went on a nightmare chase. All it took was the repetitive motion of my outstretched arms and legs to cause the seams in my cheap plastic outfit to pop. And with that, the bargain rainsuit split apart. I got soaked and I got cold. My fishing was over. What happened to me will not happen to you if you learn from my mistakes. Be ready to meet the weather with quality apparel.

Conditions in Alaska can work in exactly the opposite way as well. This happened to me on Kachemeck Bay when I booked a halibut charter outside of Homer. During the early morning hours, on our way out, I was glad I had layered up every item I had brought with me to keep me warm. It was rainy and windy and the air temperature was only 45 degrees. A mere four hours later I was anchored on a windless sea in total sunshine and the air temperature was continuing to rise. As the heat picked up so did the fishing, and by the time the temperature was near 30 degrees higher, I was cranking flat fish of that same weight from 180 feet below. Sweat poured off me. In no time, I shed everything and was soon down to my bare waist and a cotton headband as I labored to bring those brutes to the surface. Just as Alaska quickly can become cold, so too can Alaska quickly become hot. Be ready for whatever comes your way.

And do not forget those amber sunglasses. They really do brighten up dreary and rainy days, on the streams and the highways. Twilight lasts a long time at the top of the world during peak summer. Yellow lenses keep everything bright, including your disposition. Make sure that you include both types of sunglasses.

By now you have probably realized you have got a vast array of gear to bring up with you. All of it is essential and none of it is superfluous. Surprisingly, you will be able to pack it all. You *will* even be able to bring a cooler full of food at no added cost if you follow my advice. You are about to put everything into only two or three pieces of luggage that you will check from your departing city. When you get to Anchorage, they will be there waiting for you. As soon as you learn how to pack them, you will be on your way.

Things change. This sunny field of waving wildflowers is about to get drenched from the impending rain.

Chapter 11

PACKING FOR THE TRIP

Just as fishing rules and regulations surround you once you get to Alaska, so too will airline rules and regulations surround you as you pack and bring in your gear. Airlines are very specific when it comes to your checked baggage allowance. If you go past that allowance, you will have to pay a penalty. If you are flying round trip, this means you will have to pay it twice. In order to keep your trip at the economy level, you have to play by their rules. But in order to pack for your trip, you first need to discover what their rules are.

Call your carrier. Make certain you know what they allow you to bring in terms of checked baggage. Your carrier will be very specific when it comes to the number of pieces and the maximum weight of each one. Most carriers allow you to check through three pieces in combination, and this will include your carry-on luggage. Alaska is a long haul. My advice is to check all three if permitted, so that you are unencumbered on the way. The advice is the same on your return trip. Carry nothing on board, except, your bundled rods if you have to, and that shoulder-strapped vinyl cooler I mentioned earlier. I am soon to discuss its importance, but for now I will tell you that most airlines look upon that article as no more than a handbag that will slip neatly under your seat and will not count it. Take advantage of that fact.

The price of your ticket, therefore, can include up to three checked articles. These articles are your cooler, your suitcase or duffle, and perhaps your rod case. Take advantage of whatever your carrier permits you to check. What goes into your rod case and your suitcase or duffle remains unchanged both coming and going. What goes into your cooler changes completely in both directions. Your cooler will save you more money on an economy trip that you could ever imagine. Before you pack it, and the rest of your gear, there are still some more important items that you need to bring along.

ADDITIONAL ITEMS

Most of the additional things you will need are not expensive. Almost all are consumable, and you will use them up during your trip. One item, however, is costly. It plays an important role and belongs on your trip. Once you finish with it, you will return it home and continue to save money with it anyhow, so consider it an investment. All of these items are your last opportunity for localized shopping before your trip and need to be included as you pack.

Purchase several reusable gel ice packs. These blue plastic blocks measure around six-by-six inches and are two inches thick. When blue ice packs are hard frozen, they will keep your perishables cold for up to 24 hours as long as the cooler is tightly sealed. You will use these packs both coming and going. They will protect your food and your fish.

Add in a medium-sized roll of duct tape and some nylon cord. If you are not in the habit of carrying duct tape as you travel, get used to it when going to Alaska. Duct tape is so heavily used up there that Anchorage features duct tape as part of their winter carnival. Prizes are awarded for costumes made out of the stuff. You will depend on it to seal your cooler both ways. And when you are out and around, you will find other uses for it as well. The 99 cent suitcase was invented in Alaska. Hang around the luggage carrousel as you wait for your baggage in Anchorage and you will see what I mean. Locals sometimes stuff everything inside plastic garbage sacks and then just wrap duck tape all over it. Their economy luggage then checks just like a suitcase. You will smile when you see one of these packages as you wait for your gear.

You will track mud into your vehicle and it is destined to dry out and become sand and dust. Because of that, I recommend that you include a hand-held whisk broom and dust pan. An air deodorizer is also advised to keep your vehicle smelling fresh. I sometimes like to include some smaller scented candles as well. Little touches count in comfort when you are on the road.

You will need a small nylon gym bag to carry a change of clothes should you wind up in a roadside motel. It is also a convenient place to store your towels and washcloths and clean rags. If you plan on cooking on campfire coals, pick up a grilling basket. When you cut your salmon into steaks and cook them in this fashion, you will be delighted that you have it.

VACUUM PACKAGING MACHINE

This is the costly item I mentioned earlier. This machine enables you to shrink wrap your fillets in heavy-gauge plastic free of air. Fillets that are protected in this fashion will store better when iced, and will keep better when frozen. When you consider that your cooler will support upwards of 50 pounds of fillets with a market value of around $400.00, a vacuum system becomes a superior piece of technology to care for your catch. The machine is electric and easy to pack. It can be found in catalogues and in super center stores. Make sure you include a generous supply of its own plastic bags. What this machine will do for quality in preserving your catch is unrivaled. Make the investment and you will thank yourself for doing it.

FOOD AND ZIP-LOCK BAGS

The more food you can pack in your cooler, the less expensive will be your trip. Merchants in Alaska do not set out to price gouge tourists any more than they would attempt to do the same to their own local residents. The simple fact of the matter is that food prices are higher due to the freight charges involved in bringing products to Alaska's markets. With the exception of locally grown produce, most everything will be higher in cost. Whatever you can bring up will save you money if you do not have to buy it there.

Avoid canned items that are heavy and bulky. Foods such as beans, pasta, rice, sauces, soups, and powdered drinks can all be purchased in dry forms that are lightweight. You can even remove these items from their packages and pour them into plastic freezer bags. This will save you even more space as you fill your cooler. You can pack your seasonings, breading, paper goods, and aluminum foils in much the same matter. Make sure that you avoid glass containers and stick with plastic containers for all other goods.

Zip-lock bags were probably invented by that same clever person who came up with plastic garbage bags for the highway angler. They seem to make everything about your trip easier. You will depend on zip-lock bags constantly, so buy quality freezer-type bags. Always include a generous amount of pint, quart, and gallon bags. Remove them from their paper cartons and pack them into themselves. Beyond that one rectangular plastic credit card I urged you to get earlier, no other plastic products could serve you so well in Alaska as these.

Now that the major portion of your local shopping is finished, look around to see what you already own to transport your articles. If you come up short, then you will have to purchase some of these items. You have no options, and you can expect each piece I am about to point out to be packed completely full.

ROD CASE

I have previously mentioned to you the importance of this item. If your carrier permits you to check three pieces, you will use it. Rod containers are manufactured in either tube or flat case forms. I prefer the flat case, because it has room to accommodate your reels as well as your rods. If you do the tube, your reels might not fit, and if that happens, they will take up valuable space elsewhere. A flat rod-case need not be expensive. A budget case made out of hard plastic will do fine and should serve you well. If you cannot find a flat rod-case, you will be able to find a large flat gun-case. Both are similar in size. Just make sure your case has a lock on it. Break-apart rods will fit nicely into the case, and the case stores with ease in a vehicle.

I usually toss a few small elastic cords into the case before I close it up. I have discovered that in a small rental vehicle, these cords do wonders. I stretch them across the interior, near the ceiling, and they then serve as a portable rack for me to store my rigged spinning outfits when I am underway.

SUITCASE OR DUFFLE

This item will carry all of your personal clothing. Included with your apparel will be your soft-sided tackle box, backpack, fishing vest, new vacuum machine, rain gear, shoes, boots, gym bag, grilling basket, perhaps your reels, and any other things you deem important. You will pack your waders with your cooler. To all of this, now toss in the dustpan and whisk broom, drop in the *Milepost*, this book, add in all those plastic garbage bags and zip-lock bags, and you'll soon realize that you have a load of stuff to pack up.

Your suitcase, therefore, will need to be large and soft sided. This will allow you to take some of these articles out so that it can fold or compress itself for easier storage once you are underway. Some of the newer canvas duffles or trunks may be even more practical for you because they offer even more space. Don't forget that you have to keep whatever you choose to transport lightweight, and always make sure that the item you choose has a lock.

COOLER

Nothing saves you more money on an economy trip to Alaska than your cooler. Its space allows you to pack all those consumable food supplies that you have purchased at home. Not only does this save you money on the way up, it also saves you money on the way back. Once your trip is over, the empty cooler becomes filled with the fish that you get to check for free. The cooler spares you from having to buy an approved waxed container for fish. I paid out the nose for the privilege of using one of those items years ago. You will not have to.

A 48-quart ice chest will serve you nicely. Although coolers come in larger sizes, I do not recommend them because the increased space will result in increased weight. If you go over your carrier's weight limitations, they might not accept your container, and they are certain to charge you a penalty. Always respect weight limitations.

If you take the time to search around, you can find an inexpensive over-sized nylon cargo bag to put your cooler into. Lay your waders over the cooler's top, and after you zip the bag shut, use nylon cord to draw in the ends of the bag to tighten up this check-ready piece. If you do not do this, you will be forced to store your waders elsewhere. The cargo bag is a smart move. Look to find one in your catalogues, a super center store, or a luggage dealer.

Since I have recommended to you to purchase refreezable gel ice, you can take advantage of it on your way up if you so desire. The very last thing I do before I leave for the airport is pack my cooler. The bottom layer contains frozen steaks and cold-cut meats and cheeses. On top of that layer I add my frozen gel ice containers. I then insulate all of that area with my cotton hand towels and wash cloths, and continue to add in the rest of my dry food items until the chest is packed full. I then seal and wrap the cooler tightly with duct tape. All the meat stays cold until I rotate it out a day later. There is no finer way to celebrate your decision of coming to Alaska than a grilled steak cooked on your open campfire your very first night out. May my ritual become yours. Bon appetite!

SHOULDER COOLER

This was the item I recommended you carry on your flight earlier. Make sure the shoulder cooler you purchase has separate compartments. Find one that is designed with both hot and cold storage areas. Look for an additional outside pocket as well. This case allows you to carry all your important items that should never be checked. These things should always be within your reach and never in your checked bags. Here is where your camera will go, your personal toilet kit, and medicines. This type of case will hold your maps, tickets, traveler's checks, keys, sunglasses, and all other small personal articles. Even then, it'll still have room to stuff in some snacks or even a sandwich. Shoulder coolers are not expensive. If a department store near you doesn't have one, then check your major super store center. This item is invaluable and I highly recommend that you bring one.

THE DEPARTING ANGLER

Dress loosely and be comfortable for your flight. Carry your jacket and your hat. A pocket knife, corkscrew, or even nail clippers cannot be on your person or in your shoulder bag as you pass through airport security. Stuff your favorite magazine in the outside pocket and you should be ready to go. If you have followed all my advice, you are now prepared to meet just about any circumstance that lays before you. Congratulations, your next stop is Anchorage!

Chapter 12
STOCKING UP IN ANCHORAGE

After you arrive in Anchorage, your first stop will be to secure your rental vehicle. If your lease is with an agent who will pick you up, all it takes is a phone call. You will be instructed to move all your gear to the limo zone, and there you will wait until your ride comes. If you are renting a vehicle directly at the airport, you will wind up having to take your gear with you as you make your way to your agent. In either event, make sure you have tucked an ample supply of single dollar bills into your shirt pocket so that you can quickly get at them. You could have over 100 pounds of gear with you. Multiply that by the number of members of your party and the weight mounts up. Rent some baggage carts, or hire a porter, to help move your gear. Economy is always good, but sometimes it needs to be set aside for practical reasons.

Once you have secured your rental vehicle, be sure and ask your agent where a super center store is located. Anchorage has several of these stores, and regardless of what time you have arrived, there will always be some that are open. Before you hit the highways, you will have to hit the shopping center. Your adventure is going to start right in the parking lot.

The first thing you need to do is unpack your goods. You were undoubtedly very diligent in your vehicle search, and here is where it pays off. All those things you so carefully packed will now need to find new homes scattered all over the inside of your new temporary home on wheels. Organize your vehicle before you get underway. In particular, be sure to unpack all of the dry food items out of your cooler. If your rental vehicle is small and without a refrigerator, your cooler now becomes your cold storage center. Depending upon the number of members in your party, use your coolers for ice, fish, and perishable food. Segregating these cold items ensures quality and flavor. If you are by yourself, and have not included an additional ice chest in your camper package, you will need to buy an inexpensive Styrofoam cooler once you get inside the store. Once again, it is time to shop.

LICENSE

You will be able to buy your fishing license at one of the counters nearest to the fishing section. If your earlier research to the Department of Fish and Game has already resulted in your license being in your back pocket, my congratulations go to your ability to plan ahead. That same counter will usually have a copy of the state's current fishing regulations for free, so pick that up unless you have gotten so good with preplanning that it, too, is already in your possession. Ask for a tide card while you are at the counter. They will usually have it, and it is yours free for the asking.

Your nonresident sportfishing license can be bought for a variety of days. Fees will increase in proportion with usage. Dependent upon the itinerary you have planned, match your license length with your days in the field. If you have decided that you are not going to follow my advice and fish for king salmon, you will have to buy a king stamp that matches the number of days on your fishing license and your cost for each day of fishing will increase. A license can be postdated to match the days you will need it. Always carry your license with you when you are fishing. Never attempt to fish for salmon without buying your license. In all my trips to Alaska, I have never been checked, but I always play by the rules. Be certain that you do too.

FISHING EQUIPMENT

Between the catalogues and your own home sports merchandiser, you have seen it all. You will need to spend little time buying more equipment, but take a look anyhow. If you have decided to purchase an inexpensive net, look up and there it is. If you are lacking in your terminal equipment of Pixees and Russian River Flies, look down and there they are. And if you have determined that you are going to fish with bait, get a clerk to show you what you will need in terms of hooks, meshing, and processed salmon eggs. Whatever you need, get it now. Once you hit the highways, it could be a long time before you encounter another tackle department depending upon where you are going. And don't forget that the further out you are, the more costly these items can become.

CONSUMABLES

There are some items that you might wish to consider as you work your way through the food aisles. If you have rented a portable cooking stove, you will need to purchase propane fuel. If you have rented a lantern, you need to purchase more propane to power it. Lighter fluid and charcoal will also be on those aisles. So will firewood, fire starters, and box matches. You'll probably need all of these items, so stock up.

The last consumable article I recommend is a spray bottle of glass cleaning solvent. You'll soon be absolutely enthralled by your decision to come to Alaska, and won't want a dusty window or windshield to get in the way of your view. Polish your glass so clean you can take pictures through it. This is bound to happen anyhow, so you might as well have clean glass.

ANOTHER ACE TO PLAY

Take the time to make your way over to the hardware aisle. Once you get there, haul out your vehicle rental key and have a clerk make you a duplicate. Put this key in your wallet and carry it with you at all times. I sent a friend up to the Great Land one season and he made the mistake of locking his keys in his rental vehicle. He was parked in the middle of nowhere and his choice was then obvious. He had no recourse except to smash the passenger window with a rock. The replacement cost ran into the hundreds. An extra key would have cost him less than a few dollars, but he never listened to my advice, and this misfortune caused him to pay out the nose. An extra key really will give you peace of mind. Have one made.

Perishables

The only items left to buy are the ones that you couldn't pack in your cooler. If you are a breakfast person, eggs and orange juice await you. If you like to pack a lunch, then be certain to get your sandwich breads and chips. And if the evening dinner is your big meal of the day, then move on to the produce aisle.

The one supermarket area that does Alaska justice during the peak of its summer season is the fresh produce section. Vegetables and greens that grow in Alaska get daylight two-thirds of any 24-hour period. That means produce in Alaska can grow under optimum conditions that you will never see in the lower 48 states. Couple that with a soil base that is rich in volcanic ash, and you get astounding results. You can find radishes the size of plums up there. Salad greens are in abundance, and potatoes can be mammoth. The produce aisle will contain your very best values, so stock up on them as well.

The very last item you'll need is ice. Most super center stores have it available in block or crushed form. Block will last much longer, so pick up one for every cooler you intend to make cold. Crushed ice will chill your beverages, so add a bag of that as well. The rest of the ice for your trip will come to you roadside depending upon where you are. If you have not included an ice pick in your gear, buy one when you are over in the hardware aisle. Believe me, you will use it.

Take all your final shopping items and repack your coolers. Any lunch meats, cheeses, butter, or any other cold storage items will need to go into zip-locked bags so that when the ice melts they will stay dry. Use your duct tape to keep a seal on the lids of all coolers, and the ice will last longer. Keep coolers out of the sun at all times.

Hit the Road

Well, you've done it. You are equipped and ready to roll. The only thing immediately ahead of you is adventure and discovery. But don't forget what I mentioned to you earlier. If it is evening and you are tired, pull off and get some rest before you start. If you have been following all my advice, you'll probably need it anyhow. Besides, the fish will not go away. Your very first salmon is no doubt now resting behind a boulder, or in an eddy, doing the same thing you are. It is just a matter of time before you meet up with each other. By then, the two of you will be equally refreshed and full of life. The battle between you is just about guaranteed to be forthcoming.

They grow radishes the size of plums in Alaska.

Chapter 13
ON THE ROAD

Regardless of what highway system you have elected to travel upon, you will experience commonalities subject to being on the road. Just as the salmon are in the rivers and streams on their migrations, so also are the countless visitors and fishermen on all of the two-lane blacktop or gravel roads. The fish just forge ahead. The people do not. Travelers are constantly pulling over to take advantage of scenic spots, wildlife sightings, rest areas, coffee huts, fishing locations, and any other diversion or distraction along the way. Vehicles can suddenly pull off or pull onto roadways at any time. If you are driving, you must anticipate that an unknown fellow traveler can confront your vehicle with his at any time. Do not speed in Alaska and do not tailgate. Think ahead at all times.

Traffic will always be heavier during daylight than at night. Most travelers make their moves during the day, and consequently, highway conditions become more crowded during that time. You will not feel it so much if you are on one of the more lonely or moderately used roadways like the Glenn or the George Parks highways. I can guarantee you'll feel it if you are heading down the Seward Highway on your way to the Kenai Peninsula via the Sterling Highway. Congestion at these places is unavoidable.

There is only one way that you can avoid this pressure, and that is to travel at night. Fewer vehicles are on the roadways during darkness, particularly large motor homes. Tour buses are gone as well. Most of the vehicles will be smaller, and usually the drivers will be local and more experienced at driving the terrain. A night move can get you from one distant location to another with the least amount of vehicle pressure. The disadvantages of moving at night are obvious. You will experience no scenery, and driving responsibilities are more difficult. For those reasons, I do not recommend any first-timer to drive at night. If you must do so, be careful.

You can run into all types of things when you are on the road. Some are downright fun and memorable. Some are deadly and life threatening. You just never know. What I said before about your trip to Alaska, I will say again. Expect the unexpected.

CRITTERS

Wildlife in Alaska is diverse and abundant. Highway systems literally bisect their home territories. When an animal makes up its mind that a highway path is only a path for it to cross, it will cross. Sometimes these crossings are without circumstance. Sometimes they are not. Cities and towns are centered in those same territories. Just because you are a few miles out of Anchorage do not be lulled into a false sense of security thinking that animals won't cross your path. They will.

Dall sheep come right down the Chugach Mountains and onto the highway shoulder just minutes outside of Anchorage. The Seward

*A young Dall sheep runs
beside the Seward Highway.*

Highway, at this point, is a narrow twisting two-lane roadway with a mountain escarpment on one side, and a severe drop-off to a coastal fjord on the other. Road shoulders are tight, and turnoffs are few. Highway pressure is always extremely heavy. By the time an animal reaches the road, it is not the problem. The people are.

Vehicles are prone to suddenly veering off the road so that passengers can stop and take a look. Out come the cameras, then out come the people. Also, out goes good judgment. I have seen tourists needlessly endanger their lives by dashing through lines of cars on the opposite side of the highway in pursuit of a picture. I have witnessed sensible drivers lose their senses and slam on their brakes in the middle of flowing traffic. People not used to seeing animals in the wild are predictable. Common sense gets tossed out the window. This can be the norm in some places at the top of the world. When you see any

A young bull moose runs through a neighborhood in Anchorage.

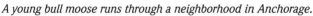

highway sign posted that indicates you are in a wildlife region, take care.

If a moose is near a roadway, be extremely careful and slow down immediately. Most crossings I have experienced are usually a cow and her calf. Out will come one, then out will come another. If this happens, remain in your vehicle for your safety, then move on. Count your sighting as good fortune and chalk it up to yet another one of those great Alaskan days.

The most memorable roadside encounter I have ever had with animals was when I was not driving, but instead walking out of a busy café adjacent to the Seward Highway. As I stepped into the parking lot, an entire family of otters was holding in order to cross the busy pavement on the opposite side of the road. When the traffic passed, I stepped out onto the clear pavement in one lane, and my friend stepped out onto the clear lane of the other. It was a unique circumstance of timing. The two us then held out our arms and blocked oncoming traffic while mother, father, and four babies sauntered across the road. No one seemed to mind, and all animals crossed safely. Unique moments like that can happen to you in the Last Frontier. I sincerely hope you have one.

DELAYS

Summer in Alaska is peak time for everything. It is also peak time for the Department of Transportation to do their thing, and that is repairing or rebuilding roads. Do not be surprised if somewhere during your trip traffic comes to a complete stop. It does and it will. When that happens, it usually means that somewhere ahead of you, road construction is taking place. Your wait may be as short as five minutes or as long as half an hour. It all depends on where you are, and what is happening during the time you are there. You cannot fight it. Shut off your engine and take a moment to smell the flowers. You will soon be back underway.

A family of river otters cross the highway near Seward.

SURFACE CONDITIONS

Just because your highway map shows a thin black line that indicates pavement, do not count on it. Road surfaces are subject to change. Changes usually take place during construction. I was crossing the Glenn Highway during one trip when suddenly the highway ended and there was nothing but dirt, rocks, and gravel for five miles. If that was not enough, it was also raining. Add to that, potholes and ruts that were a foot deep and filed with water. Heavy highway excavating equipment was scattered everywhere, and tiny detours around mounds of dumped fill were numerous. I had to creep for half an hour just to make it through.

When I was there, that same highway had been subjected to permafrost damages. The intermix of frozen and warmed land, topped by pavement, had caused the asphalt surface to buckle and heave. Parts of the highway turned into roller coaster rides that same day.

Needless to say, I wound up behind schedule. Always give yourself a little more time on the road than what your research says it will take to drive it. You never know what you are going to run into. As a matter of fact, you may even run into some things along the side of the road that you can use for free.

FREE WOOD AND ICE

I keep a sharp eye out when I am on the road. Since I frequently camp, I know that an evening fire and firewood to fuel it, will always be part of my ritual. Public-use campgrounds are usually devoid of firewood. Areas adjacent to campsites have been scoured and picked clean. Wood you burn then becomes wood you have to buy. I learned a long time ago that free wood is usually lying around in areas not near campgrounds. All you have to do

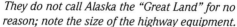

They do not call Alaska the "Great Land" for no reason; note the size of the highway equipment.

is simply slow down a little when on the road and take the time to look. You'll be surprised.

If you happen to be in an area near a glacier, you may have another free opportunity. For years, I used to fill my fish coolers with the floating ice that littered the shoreline of Portage Glacier just south of Anchorage. Every trip down the Kenai started out with crystal-clear chunks of ice thousands of years old. All it took was a few minutes and the ice pick. And besides, it was fun, too. I do not know where you are destined to wind up, but if it is next to ice, it's yours for free.

OTHER CONDITIONS

The last variables you will confront on the road are dust, gravel and weather. If you drive on improved gravel roads, the by-product will be the dust caked all over your vehicle. That is why I recommended you buy the glass cleaner back in Anchorage. You will be glad you have it. Keep your windows and mirrors clean for safety at all times.

Gravel roads also throw rocks, and rocks crack windshields. There is little you can do to prevent this. Once it even happened to me. I paid only the deductible because I had listened to my insurance agent and had planned for the unforeseen.

Your final variable is the weather. Expect anything. Adjust your driving to those conditions. It actually snowed on me once during July when I was on the road. After that circumstance, I realized I had seen it all. Rain, wind, fog, ice, snow, mud, and perfect sunshine all await you when you hit the road in Alaska.

LOOKING AHEAD

Now that you know how to deal with the variables confronting you, it's time to think about two more variables that you will have to deal with when you are parked. You are soon to confront your fellow angler, and you are soon to confront your fish. As you follow my advice, you will learn how to play them both with equal success.

A glacier works its way down the mountain near a campsite at Portage.

Chapter 14
TECHNIQUE AND ETIQUETTE

I have advised you to fish for salmon with a spinning rod and an open-faced spinning reel because that combination is the most inexpensive and practical presentation you can use. All three terminals can be used on the end of the line of a spinning outfit. You can go from spoon, to fly, or to bait in a matter of minutes. You can switch out spools and exchange lines in a matter of seconds. The moment you step into a crowded bank-fishery you will understand the reasoning behind these recommendations. Many of your fellow anglers will be using equipment similar to yours. Spinning is the practical way to go.

Chances are that you are already skilled in spinfishing techniques. This certainly will help you. But chances also are that you have never fished for salmon in a river or stream before in your life. Wade fishing for salmon will be unlike anything you have ever done before. Spinning in current is very unlike spinning in a still body of water. Fighting fish in current is unlike fighting fish in stillwaters. Even standing knee to thigh deep in moderate- to fast-flowing water will be a first for many of you.

Walking in fast-moving water without falling down requires common sense and skill. The deeper and faster the water, the greater the risk of a fall. Most areas are easy. You will be able to stand right at the bank's edge and cast, and you will seldom be in water over your knees. But some areas are tougher, and you will have to walk and then wade into water in order to put yourself in a desireable casting area. This is where you must use your head before you start to fish.

WADING

Walk slowly when you wade. Look down and look ahead as you step at all times. You are probably in clear water, so take advantage of the clarity to help you see where you are going. Take short steps, and take your time. This assists you in helping to establish your balance. Avoid stepping up onto boulders or large rocks. They have a tendency to be slippery, so go around them. If you are wearing hip waders go no deeper than beyond your knees. If you are wearing chest waders, go no deeper than beyond your waist. The moment you walk into a situation where you think you have encountered risk, back out of it immediately.

Anglers fishing together sometimes can pair up and use each other for balance in some wading situations. Hanging on to each other is recognized as a technique if the going gets swift. At other times, a long branch or a folding wading stick can be used to assist those going solo. How you handle wading in moving water will be dependent upon where you are and who you are with.

Remember that unfortunate angler who locked his keys in the car and had to smash the window glass? This was the same guy who did not listen to me about my tips on wading. He went down in a cold-water river because he was standing too deep. There was no doubt he was in a choice spot, but the moment he moved out of it to play his hooked salmon, things were not so choice. He slipped, dropped his pole, and went under. Thankfully he had the knowledge to roll on his back and point his boots down the stream. He then used both his arms to propel himself to the shallows where he could stand. At least he did not panic. But he could have drowned. Believe me, a fish is not worth it. Never wade at the edge of common sense.

When you fish for salmon, you are going to go at it in either crowded or uncrowded conditions. If there are few fishermen, there are few rules. If there are many fishermen, there are many rules. The problem is, none of these rules are written. Your fellow angler is depending on you to abide by rules that he assumes you already know. And since you have not been there before, let me point them out to you.

COMBAT FISHING

I mentioned this to you earlier. When some of the greatest fishing on Earth

Combat fishing.

presents itself, this kind of fishing is unavoidable, and you are getting ready to step right into it. Before you do so, please follow these recommendations:

1. Scout around outside the zone before you start. Look over the entire fishing area carefully. You may be able to avoid a zone of heavy pressure by hiking up or downstream from where everybody is. This sometimes does work. If this is impossibile, then you must join your fellow anglers where they are.

2. Scout around inside the zone. Check the stringers of the anglers in front of you. If they are full, or just about full, chances are good that some fishermen will soon be leaving. Communicate with the angler when you see this as a possibility. Wait until they leave, and then step in.

3. Step into the zone if you have to. If you cannot go around them, and you cannot wait them out, then it is your right to step in. Look up and down the entire line and find the spot with the least density. Make sure that when you walk into your spot you know what you're doing. Crashing a tight line is not advised for the inexperienced angler.

When you are fishing in a combat zone there are some things you should and should not do. Always assist anyone if they ask for your help. This is just being friendly. If you tangle up with another angler, quickly determine who untangles and get on with it. Never cut your neighbors terminal unless you cannot untangle it. If severe knots require a cut, let it be known,

and then personally return the lure to the fisherman.

When your neighbor has a fish on, retrieve your line and step aside to give him room to play his fish. What you do for him, he will do for you. Once the fish has been landed, resume your casting.

Never take an angler's spot who is on the shore landing or stringing a fish. Fishermen consider that tantamount to theft up there, so do not do it. If any angler has left his spot to return to his tackle box or backpack, respect that space as well. If the angler is on the bank eating lunch or enjoying a cold one, then that spot is now up for grabs.

Please do not play catch-and-release in a crowded combat zone. The only reason some fishermen endure these tight conditions is to harvest fish. Take your limit, then step out to give

This is what a tight line of combat fishing looks like.

the other fishermen a chance. Catch-and-release is recognized as a deserving technique in almost any other spot, except where people are trying to put meat on the table. Take the time to look around at other anglers who are poorer than you, and you will understand what I mean.

Stay in harmony with your neighbors. Once you edge up next to them, you'll discover that everyone follows a kind of rhythm based upon the length and timing of their casts as they direct their casts upstream. Take a moment to watch and learn. When you feel the timing is right, direct your cast.

Combat fishing is productive, but it is linked with responsibility and common courtesy. I am always amazed to see so many perfect strangers working so well next to one another. This is usually the norm up there. If by some misfortune you have wound up next to someone who is critical and argumentative, leave that area and find another one. Life is just too short. In all my years to the Great Land this has never happened to me. I hope it never happens to you either.

Rigging Your Terminal Gear

Since I have recommended that everything you will need to catch salmon comes either from the Pixie Spoon, Russian River Fly, or baited salmon hook, all you need to know is how to configure them with lead, swivel, and leader. It really is quite simple.

Spoon

If you are casting with a spoon, you have two choices. You can use a leader or you can omit it. If you are building a leader, all you need to do is cut

an 18-inch segment from your spool. Attach one end to your barrel swivel, and then tie the other end to your spoon. If you are fishing without a leader, all you do is tie a snap swivel to the end of your line and then snap in your spoon. Lead is traditionally not used in conjunction with spoons. The weight of the spoon carries the cast. I have observed little difference in results with either spoon attachment.

Cast your spoon upstream and coordinate your retrieve so that your line stays tight. As the current washes your spoon downstream, point your rod tip in the same direction. Try to keep your spoon as deep as possible. Keep your rod tip low. When a salmon strikes your lure, the bite will be dramatic and very obvious. Immediately set your hook hard and the fight is on.

Fly

If you are casting with a fly, you must build a leader accompanied by lead. Lead is used to cast the fly and then sink it to the bottom. The current washes the lead and fly downstream. To build a leader, all you need do is cut an 18-inch segment from your spool. Attach one end to your barrel swivel, and then tie the other end to your fly. Before you attach this segment to your spooled line, determine what you are going to use for lead. The weight is attached directly above the swivel. You will have to adjust your lead weight so that your fly bounces on the bottom with the wash of the current. Too much weight will stall it. Too little weight will not bring it down. Look around and see what your fellow anglers are using to help you with your decision.

Cast your fly upstream and coordinate your retrieve so that your line stays tight. As the current washes your lead and fly downstream, point your rod tip in the same direction. Try to keep your fly as deep as possible. Keep your rod tip low. When a salmon strikes your fly the bite will be undramatic and not obvious. It will only feel like a gentle tug. Immediately set your hook by jerking your rod tip upwards in a hard thrust. Spin fishing with a fly is going to be new to you. It takes some practice to be able to distinguish between the bumping of your lead and the tugging of a fish. The key to success is to always keep your line tight, and never hesitate to set the hook.

BAITED HOOK

If you are casting with bait, you must build a leader accompanied by lead. Lead will be used to cast the bait and then sink it to the bottom. Lead weights can vary. Heavy ones hold the bait on the bottom motionless until a salmon picks it up. Lighter ones allow the bait to roll until it comes in contact with the fish. Either work, but are dependent upon the conditions of where you are. To build the leader, all you need do is cut an 18-inch segment from your spool. Attach one end to your barrel swivel, then tie the other end to your salmon hook. Before you attach this segment to your line, determine what you are going to use in lead weight and attach that to your spooled line above the swivel.

Use your fillet knife to cut about a 1- to 2-inch segment of salmon eggs. Thread this segment onto your hook and then use fabric meshing to wrap the eggs and hold them in place. Processed salmon eggs are far more durable than fresh roe.

They will hold up longer in the current, and are advised for swift conditions.

When you cast your bait and it settles to the bottom, it will either roll or stay in place depending on both the weight of the lead and the strength of the current. In every circumstance, though, the key is to keep your line tight at all times, and keep your rod tip low. When a salmon picks up your bait, the bite will either be dramatic or just a series of soft tugs. In either circumstance, set your hook hard.

Regardless of what terminal choice you have selected, there is something in common with all three presentations that is very important. Keep your hooks sharp. A dull hook works just about as well as a dull fillet knife, both will do you an injustice. The sharper the hook, the better your results.

FISH ON!

This is why you came to Alaska. The moment you hook your very first salmon, your heart will leap up and grab you by the throat. I have fished all over North America, and seldom have I encountered a species that has demonstrated as much heart as they have. Pound for pound, they are among the toughest fighters.

If your surrounding conditions allow you to play your fish, then by all means, do so. Slow-moving water and light crowd pressure will contribute to this opportunity. Let the fish tire itself out before bringing it to shore. Your rod, reel, and line will do you justice as you pump your fish and wear it down. But do not forget that reverse conditions require the opposite strategy. There is not much room to wear your salmon down in a combat zone. Bring your fish in immediately. This is your responsibility.

Once you have caught your limit, your daily harvest is over. Do not violate fishing regulations, and make certain that you read the rules and follow them. You may not have seen them, but in some of those crowds of fellow anglers are the fish cops. The Department of Fish and Game takes everything about management and enforcement very seriously. Conservation officers can be anywhere at any time. They can be in uniform or they can be undercover. Violations are costly and punitive. The greatest fishery on Earth is managed and policed, and that is why it is so great. Make certain that you are always a well-behaved guest.

CATCH-AND-RELEASE

Just because your harvest quota is over, your fishing day is not. You are more than welcome to play catch-and-release in Alaska so long as you follow guidelines to ensure releasing fish unharmed back into the water. Don't do this with baited hooks, do this only with flies or spoons. If you are using a fly, take your needlenose pliers and bend down the barb on the hook. If you are using a spoon with a treble hook, switch out the hook and replace it with a single salmon hook and then bend down the barb. Once you have taken care of these responsibilities, you can play the game until your arms darn near fall off.

Play your hooked salmon carefully, but not to the point of complete exhaustion. As your fish nears the shore, enter the water so that you can cradle the fish under its belly. Grasp it around the tail if necessary, but

never net it or drag it onto shore. Always keep the fish in the water. Once your fish is subdued, use your pliers to carefully remove the hook. Then transfer the fish to deeper water and gently let it go.

I have played catch-and-release for hours in this manner. It never bores me, but it does wear me out. By the way, there is even a little added bonus to this game. Many salmon you catch will have been hooked by others. It is not unusual to land salmon with flies stuck all over them due to battles that occured before the fish reached you. Any fly you remove is yours free for the taking. I once landed a humpy from hell that had three flies stuck in his back. That pink salmon was a gift from heaven. I even waved goodbye and thanked him for the five dollars worth of terminal as I set him free.

WRAPPING UP YOUR DAY

As your fishing ends, make certain that you have taken care of your responsibilities. Anything that has served to assist you gets packed out. Be certain that any trash that you have generated leaves with you. If you have cut fish beside the stream, all the entrails and remaining carcasses go right back into the water to serve as nutrients for future fish. Leave everything as it was and continue on your way.

By now you are catching fish. I can almost almost guarantee that by the added weight on your back and the bulge of your pack. Now that you have them, you have even more responsibility in preserving what you have caught. Taking proper care of your fish is imperative. The next section shows you how.

Catching your salmon is one thing; bringing it home is another. You have an ice chest, gel ice, fillet knives, plastic bags, and a vacuum-packing machine to assist you in this task. You also have ice to help keep your catch cold along the way. You have every right to take these prizes home with you, but the moment you pull your fish from the stream, you're faced with the responsibility of taking care of it. This responsibility will not change until your fish are home and packed securely in your freezer. Although you have miles to go between here and there, it can all still be fun and rewarding along the way.

Fish is a highly perishable food item. When it is raw and uncooked, it must be taken care of immediately or it will quickly spoil. Air, time, and temperature are the elements that you must control in order to bring what you have caught safely home. If you have followed my advice in what to bring on your trip to Alaska, you are now equipped and prepared to deal with this obligation.

You have several options as to what you can do with your salmon while you are on the road. You can eat your catch, you can preserve your catch and take it home, or you can have your catch commercially processed and shipped home later. All three are terrific options. Two will not cost you a cent and are absolutely free, and the other one, although

Tom Krause displays of nice catch of silver salmon
about to be filleted on a log and a piece of drift wood.

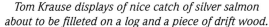

costly, will still save you money. I recommend that you do them all. Each will contribute to great Alaskan memories.

Regardless of what choices you make, you are immediately faced with decisions the moment you call it a day and return to your stringer. Whole fish will be strung on it, and you must now decide what you are going to do with them. Depending on your intent, fish will either have to be filleted or eviscerated, and then packed out.

EATING YOUR CATCH

You may not have noticed it, but when I advised you about stocking up in Anchorage, nothing was mentioned about your purchasing any food item to serve as your main course for the evening meal. That was a deliberate omission. Outside of the frozen food I advised you to bring, I was counting on you to have salmon as your main course. I certainly hope this is the case. No fish eats finer than what you catch, and this is especially true in Alaska.

If you are at the stringer and you plan on eating your catch, then take a look around before you pull your fillet knife from its sheath. Field dressing salmon is the norm up there, and several of the more crowded areas even have stainless cleaning tables set up in the streams. These

A pair of anglers utilize a fish-cleaning station set up on the Russian River.

areas make filleting your catch easy, so use them if they are around. Should you be in an area less traveled, then look for a fallen log to set your fish. At the very least, lay your salmon on top of a boulder or down in the grass. Never cut on sand; the reason should be obvious.

Leave the skin on your fillets. All entrails and carcasses go back into the stream. Pull your zip-locks out of your pack and zip your prize shut. Back into the pack goes your dinner. You are off. It is that easy.

Freshly prepared salmon is wonderful. I am not about to throw a recipe at you, but I will mention of something I always do. When I pack for my trip, I always include a generous amount of heavy-duty tin foil. One of the ways that I enjoy salmon is to have it smoked. If you have an ample supply of foil, you can always find a way to rig up your campfire to become a mini smokehouse.

I usually do this with hot coals and hardwood scraps that have been soaked in water. By now, you should know me well enough to have figured out that before I left the stream, I took a few minutes to look around to find my wood for smoking. It was waiting there for me, already pre-soaked, and all I had to do was pick it up. Fresh-smoked salmon is delicious either hot or cold.

I am not the only one who plans ahead. Many Asians are particularly fond of fish, both cooked and raw, and it has been a part of their diet for centuries. When I was on the Kenai River one afternoon I chanced upon this circumstance. Perched on the bank, next to the flowing river, was an Asian family having a picnic. They were dining on china with linen and had brought sauces and pre-cooked rice. Centered on their outstretched blanket was a picnic basket that was topped by a freshly cut bouquet of Alaskan fireweed stuffed into an empty bottle of rice wine. As I looked down to the adjacent river's edge, I could see a single red salmon still on the stringer with one side missing. When the happy family held up their bowls and chopsticks and pointed to the river, I could not help but smile. I bet they had planned for that moment for months. Their meal could not have been fresher, the fish was only minutes old.

PRESERVING YOUR CATCH

This option is your entitlement. Your license fee allows you a daily quota of salmon. You have paid for the right to take your fish home for every day you fish, and I will show you how to do it. But think about the circumstances of those rights before you begin exercising them. A red-hot fishery at the start of a seven-day trip can fill a cooler fast. Unless you are prepared to pay to have your excess fish commercially processed, you might want to slow down. This is an important decision to make. If the fishing is unusually good, be prepared to deal with this fact.

If you are at the stringer and you plan on freezing and preserving your catch, then begin by following the same procedure as if you were going to consume it. Cut your fish, leave the skin on, zip it in plastic, put it in your backpack, and walk out. Once you get to your vehicle, put your bagged fillets in your iced cooler and seal it with duct tape.

Red salmon is the most revered and highly prized flesh in all of Alaska's salmon species.

Keep your cooler out of the sun and avoid opening the lid later just to look inside. Always keep your fish as cold as possible.

Your next responsibility is to vacuum process your fillets. This removes the air and helps protect your fish until you can get a freeze on them. Remove the skin. Fillet out any gray areas of fat. Pat the fillets dry and then vacuum process them with your machine.

You will need electricity in order to do this. That is why I stagger my campground stays between roadside motels with a kitchen. As I freshen up between campgrounds, I know I will have the opportunity to shrink-wrap and freeze my fish, plus refreeze the gel ice as well. I recommend that you do this, but if not, you do have some options.

Look around your campground. Your host might have power, or a neighboring motor home might be running its generator. All you have to do is be polite and ask. Alaska is full of friendly people. Chances are they will not turn you down. If your immediate area is without power, then you will have to wait until you hit the road. Once you are out, your possibilities are endless. Once again, just be polite and ask. At the very least, once you get near a town, you can at least toss in a load of laundry and probably shrink-wrap your fish right there. In any event, get it done. The sooner you do it, the better your salmon will keep.

There are some highway businesses that offer freezer space you can rent while you are on the road. The *Milepost* will identify the establishments that will be on your highway system. If you know you will be returning to their location, you can buy into these services. This is recommended if you have a cooler full of your own filleted and shrunk-wrapped fish. Not only does it ensure that your catch has a hard freeze on it before you return home, but it also reopens your cooler for space you will need if you plan on bringing back more whole fish for commercial processing.

When I do the double-highway trip, I always plan on unloading an entire cooler right in Anchorage. I rent a locker from a processor to freeze what I have harvested from the first highway. I then return to him with my whole fish caught from the second highway. This works out perfectly. If you elect to do this, make certain that you arrive during regular business hours. Once again, timing is critical.

PROCESSING YOUR CATCH

This is the last option available to you. The bad news is that this option costs. The good news is that this option can save you money. The better news is that this option removes the responsibility of your having to care for your fish aside from delivering it to the processor. The outstanding news is that commercially processed salmon is considered to be the finest-eating fish in the world. Commercial processing results in an absolute gourmet fish product that you cannot duplicate. It is worth every cent.

A salmon can be processed in one of three ways. It can be kippered, it can be rendered into lox, or it can be turned into jerky. All three look different. All three taste different. All three cost about the same. Every way is excellent. Smoke processing takes several weeks to accomplish. Dependent upon the selection, the fish may be subjected to a brine soaking for flavor, and then subjected to a peri-

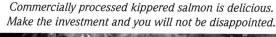

Commercially processed kippered salmon is delicious.
Make the investment and you will not be disappointed.